Designed by Philip Clucas
Produced by Ted Smart and David Gibbon

CLB 1500
© 1986 Text: Colour Library Books Ltd., Guildford, Surrey, England.
© 1986 Illustrations: Chuck Solomon, Major League Baseball Promotion Corp.
   and Focus on Sport.
Text filmsetting by Acesetters Ltd., Richmond, Surrey, England.
All rights reserved.
1986 edition published by Crescent Books, distributed by Crown Publishers, Inc.
Printed in Spain.
ISBN 0 517 601907
h g f e d c b a

To Mom and Dad, for instilling the
   inspiration which made this work
      possible.

THE WORLD OF
MAJOR LEAGUE
BASEBALL

Paul Fichtenbaum

CRESCENT BOOKS
NEW YORK

CONTENTS

FOREWORD
by SHANE RAWLEY

Who is your favorite baseball player? Is it Mattingly, Guidry, Schmidt, or Gooden? Or was it Banks, Aaron, or could it have been Ruth, or even Cobb.

Are you kidding? It can't be any of those players. Let's face it, how many of you Cardinal fans felt the ball smack the bat when Jack Clark hit his home run against the Dodgers to put them in the World Series? And how many of you Dodger fans said, "How could he throw a pitch like that!"? What about you Met fans. Don't you put a little extra in your yell when Gooden has two strikes on the batter? And how did you feel when they strike out? I know, as if you threw the pitch.

When you get right down to it, your favorite baseball player has to be you. That's what baseball is all about, being a part of your favorite team. To feel great when Pete Rose slides head first into second base only inches ahead of the throw. To get mad when Jim Rice hits into his thirty-second double play of the season. All of these exciting moments are what make you feel a part of Major League Baseball.

How many of you cried when you heard that Lou Gehrig was ending his career so tragically? Or when you got the news that Pete Redfern had become paralyzed and will be lucky to walk again, much less pitch in the Big Leagues.

Did you laugh when Bob Uecker thought his free tickets were in the "frrront row!"? How about the night Mike Schmidt strolled out to first base with a wig on under his baseball cap. Do you remember how you felt?

Without you sitting in those centerfield bleachers in Wrigley Field yelling for Sutcliffe to pitch another shutout, or you people in the "frrront row" at Anaheim Stadium wanting Reggie to hit another home run, our job becomes meaningless.

So sit back in your favorite chair, grab a hot dog and soda, then page through this enjoyable book. Put your favorite player, that's you, inside these photos reliving the past baseball season. Then, when you're finished, close the book and look forward to a new and fresh beginning of another unforgettable year with the boys of summer. Because without you, our favorite players, there is no Major League Baseball.

Cesar Cedeno (facing page) helped the Cards to a World Series berth. Keith Hernandez (below) won another Gold Glove at first base.

INTRODUCTION

Ever since Abner Doubleday placed the bases 90 feet apart and the pitching mound 60 feet 6 inches away from home plate more than 100 years ago, baseball has been known as the national pastime. Kids would play it on street corners or in sandlots, and the family would gather around the radio and tune in to their favorite team, their favorite hero. The Babe was the Babe, the Yankees were the best and bars were places where Giants and Dodgers fans would argue the merits of their team.

But a lot has changed since the halcyon years of baseball. The season has stretched from just the warmth of summer to the frigidness of early spring and fall. Today there are free agents, a misnomer if there ever was one. There is television and there are drugs and there are strikes. Through it all, baseball has survived and, surprisingly, baseball has become even more popular. And while some of the deviations in the game have been welcomed, and some frowned upon, many have occurred over the past two decades.

The American and National League have taken separate identities in the way the game is played. The senior circuit is the home of spacious, artificial turf stadiums. Of the 12 teams in the league, half play in the new parks, the ones with the carpeted floors, the cavernous power alleys and the distant fences. The emphasis, clearly, is away from power and towards speed. Not only on the basepaths and in the outfield, but on the mound, where the fastballs are fast and fastballs are also plentiful.

The American League is the home of the old stadiums, the cozy ballparks with the short porch in rightfield or the Green Monster. It is the league of the designated hitter, a league of older players and older pitchers who try the patience of the batters with their assortment of breaking balls.

In the National League, managers will play for one run, have the steal sign on when it's least expected and make sure the outfielders are at least as fast as Carl Lewis. Witness the National League champion St. Louis Cardinals.

"In the National League you have to play the lines differently because the gaps are deeper and the ball gets there quicker," said Yankees outfielder Ken Griffey, a former N.L. player. "In the N.L. you've got to run. You don't have to sit back and wait if you have speed. You can manufacture a run if you have speed."

In the junior circuit, the focus is on the big inning, the three-run homer and the off-speed pitch. With the advent of the designated hitter in 1973, A.L. teams stack their lineup with big hitters who can't run. Well, they can do the home run trot.

"Pitchers don't want to give in to hitters in a hitters' ballpark," says Houston's pitching coach Jerry Walker.

"In a place like Fenway Park," says Alan Ashby, a veteran of both leagues, "pitchers are going to pitch more carefully than they would in the Astrodome."

And while both leagues practice a different style of play, one thing is certain. It's still baseball, the national pastime.

The Detroit Tigers' dynamic duo (above left) of Lance Parrish and Kirk Gibson have much to celebrate in the smaller A.L. parks. Dwight Gooden (facing page) is a quintessential example of the N.L.'s power pitchers.

ROSE THE TY-BREAKER

February 13, 1985: Pete Rose, at a promotional luncheon at New York's Tavern on the Green, is asked to name the date on which he will break Ty Cobb's record of 4191 hits in a career. In the usual Pete Rose style, he studies the extra-large calendar on display, sees the month of September is highlighted and says "Well, for one thing, you've got the wrong month." Later he predicts the historic date to be August 26. "OK, so I was wrong," he says after he breaks the record on September 11 at Cincinnati's Riverfront Stadium, "Sue me."

Such is Pete Rose. Brash, cocky, intense. Never one to hide from his mistakes and never one to hide from his accomplishments. "You know the three stats I'm most proud of that aren't in the press guide? I got the highest average of games played per season, the highest average of hits per season and the highest average of 600 at bats per season. Did you know I played in more winning games than Joe DiMaggio? Consistency."

Consistency has been the hallmark of Pete Rose since he broke into the major leagues in 1963. The 44-year-old Reds player/manager, who is heading into his 24th major league season, owns enough records and has won enough awards to fill every den in Smalltown U.S.A. Consider this: most games, most at bats, most seasons 200 or more hits, most consecutive seasons 100 or more hits, most seasons with 600 or more at bats, fifteen seasons with an average of .300 or better and a career average of .305.

Still some skeptics figure since Rose played more games than Cobb, the record should be in the books with an asterisk. Just don't tell that to Pete Rose. "Hey, he played 24 years, didn't he? Evidently, he must have taken too many games off. Consistency is the name of the game. I might be first in hits, but I'm also first in making outs. Look at (Mickey) Mantle, fifteen hundred and something strikeouts. That means he was there every day.

"I thought people liked to see me break the record because I play like the old-time ballplayer. I thought everybody hated Ty Cobb. I keep reading where nobody came to his funeral."

***

April 8, 1985: Opening Day. The Reds traditionally begin the major league

Pete Rose (above and left) takes time out to chat while also showing the form that produced the record-breaking hit (facing page).

season by hosting the first game. Today is no different. The only difference is that Pete Rose the manager, announces that Pete Rose the player will platoon with a younger man, Tony Perez (43). No problem. The Montreal Expos pitch

righthander Steve Rogers. Rose starts and promptly doubles and singles for hits number 4098 and 4099. Only 92 to Ty.

April 10, 1985: another historic milestone. Hit number 4100. This time a single off Bill Gullickson.

***

Pete Rose makes his pro debut on June 25, 1960 as a 19-year-old in the New York-Penn League. Two singles, an RBI, in five at bats. From the very first game, people notice the different style of play. A local newspaper at the time reports that Rose is an aggressive ballplayer with a chance to be a good hitter.

His first season produces a modest .277 batting average and immodest 36 errors at second base. "The reports on me back in Cincinnati weren't too good," he recalls, "but at the end of the year the fans voted me the most popular player."

Rose steadily climbs in the Reds organization, hitting .331 in 1961, and .330 a year later in Macon in the Class A Sally League. Finally, the kid who upsets

veterans by running out walks and sliding head first, lands in the major leagues. In his first full year, Rose bats .273 and wins the Rookie-of-the-Year award. "There are three things I wanted to do in baseball," Rose says, "and that's get base hits, score runs and win games."

As comedian Steven Wright says, "You can't have everything; where would you put it?" Pete Rose, the man who has just about everything, is looking for a spot.

***

* 1,025 hits in stadiums that no longer exist.

* Hits off pitchers from 13 different countries.

* Six hits off Ivy Leaguers.

* 155 hits off 300-game winners.

* 131 hits off Hall-of-Famers.

* 192 hits off brother sets.

* 7 hits off convicts.

accomplishments in baseball. In spring training of his second season, Rose walks into camp and proclaims that he will make the all-star team and lead the Reds to a pennant. It seems Rose hasn't heard of the sophomore jinx.

He begins the season in a slump and by mid-June still hasn't recovered. Batting .214 and sitting on the bench, Rose seeks the help of his uncle, who promptly tells him to lower his hands and attack the ball. As a result, Rose finishes strongly and

August 17, 1985: Rose gets three hits against Houston in the Astrodome to raise his total 4175. Only 16 for a tie, 17 for the Ty-breaker. Two of the hits come at the expense of 40-year-old Joe Niekro, a victim 39 times in his career. That's nothing compared to his older brother Phil, who has allowed Rose 64 hits, most of any of the 628 pitchers Rose has hit off. That prompts Rose to say "I've gotten more than 100 hits off the Niekros. I just wish she'd had triplets."

Those aren't the only incredible numbers Rose has compiled. A peek into the records shows Rose has:

* 19 hits off club vice presidents (Dallas Green of the Cubs and Bill Stoneman of the Expos).

* 6 hits off a pitcher born after he first went to bat in the major leagues (Dwight Gooden).

* 29 hits off dentists (Dr. Jim Lonborg and Dr. Steve Arlin).

* 9 hits off orthopedic surgeons (Dr. Ron Taylor and Dr. George Medich).

***

After winning the rookie award Pete Rose is ready for bigger

Pete Rose (facing page) shows his record-breaking form. Phil Niekro (above left) and Ron Darling (above) both contributed to Rose's hit collection.

winds up hitting .269, still the third-lowest average of his career.

That sophomore season proves to be one of the few stumbling blocks in his career. Nine consecutive seasons of .300 average or better follow, along with three World Series rings in six trips to the Fall Classic and eight appearances in the league championship series.

But things are not always smooth. In the 1970 all-star game with 50,000

witnesses in person and millions more on TV, the hard-nosed Rose reinforces his nickname of Charlie Hustle by steamrolling rookie catcher Ray Fosse in a home-plate collision. Three years later, Rose solidifies his rough and tumble image even more when he slides hard into second base and tangles with 5-9, 160-pound Mets shortstop Bud Harrelson during the third game of the championship series. A bench-clearing brawl ensues and Rose finds himself being pelted with rocks and bottles from Shea Stadium faithful.

"I won't forget that day," says Harrelson, now a Mets coach. "He'd do anything he could to get his team going. I knew it then and I know it now. And I respect it."

***

September 8, 1985: the scene, Chicago's Wrigley Field. Rose's hit total is now 4189 after connecting for career home run number 160 off Cubs rookie Derek Botelho the day before. Rose is planning to sit today because Chicago is scheduled to pitch lefthander Steve Trout. But early Sunday morning it is learned that Trout skidded on a patch of gravel riding his bicycle and injured his left shoulder. Enter Reggie Patterson, a rookie righthander. Enter Rose, who will now play and go after the record.

On the first pitch of his first at bat, Rose pokes a single to left field. Hit number 4190. In the fifth, Patterson throws two quick strikes before evening the count. "The next one was a sinking fastball just off the corner of the plate," Rose said. "At 3-2 I knew I'd get a fastball. He gave me one slightly off the plate and I pulled it into rightfield." Hit number 4191. Move over, Ty, you've got some company at the top.

"I was going to go over and shake his hand, but I stopped," Patterson said. "I don't know why. It was a history-making event that people wanted to see."

Now comes the true test of Rose's character. With at least two more at bats in the ballgame, Rose can easily remove himself from the lineup, saving his record-breaking hit for the home crowd at Riverfront on Tuesday. Rose never even considers it.

"When I got the hit, Dave Parker came up to me and said, 'Don't do it, don't do it.' I said, 'I gotta. We're trying to win the game.' He said, 'You're going to make my all-gutty team when I retire.'"

Top of the seventh. Rose leads off against reliever Lary Sorenson. With the entire crowd of 28,269 on its feet, Rose works the count to 2-2 before smashing a hard grounder to shortstop Shawon Dunston.

"It was a real special moment," said Sorenson. "I got to pitch on Carl

each time Rose steps to the plate.

Before the game, Rose discusses the previous evening's Nightline TV show, in which Cobbs' son defends his father's record. "There's no way of comparing a player today against a Babe Ruth or Ty Cobb," he said. "I have a lot of admiration for the old-time player. It's hard to make comparisons. They say we play more games, the travel was better in one era. It's impossible. I think one thing people don't think about is the amount of speed there is in the outfields today. Ever try to hit a ball through the gap between Vince Coleman and Willie McGee? I know Ty Cobb missed about 500 games. Thank goodness. You guys would be hanging around here a lot longer."

Rose makes them hang around just a little longer. Four times he comes up and four times he makes out against Padres pitchers LaMarr Hoyt and Lance McCullers. Rose pops out to shortstop in his first time up before lofting a lazy fly to leftfielder Carmelo Martinez his second trip. His other two at bats also ended with fly ball outs.

History will have to wait only one more day.

September 11, 1985: how ironic it is. On the 57th anniversary of Ty Cobb's last swing in the big leagues, Pete Rose breaks the all-time hit record with a looping, soft single to left field off pitcher Eric Show. Hit number 4192. The Big Knock, as Pete Rose liked to call it.

The celebration lasts about seven minutes. Long enough for Pete Rose, Mr. Macho, the man who likes to hide his emotion, to stand at first base and cry like a baby.

"I was all right until I looked up and then I saw my dad there with Ty Cobb and that took care of me."

"I've never seen him cry before," said long-time teammate Tony Perez. "Never, never. He was crying so much he was making everybody feel mushy inside. It really got to him. We broke down and cried on the bench."

Before they could, Rose is showered with ovations and gifts. Ovations from the sellout crowd at Riverfront Stadium. Gifts from Reds owner Marge Schott. The first is a great big bearhug right at first base. The second, a custom-made red Corvette, wheeled in from centerfield. He tipped his hat several times to the crowd before a final emotional embrace from his son Petey.

After the game, an emotionally drawn Pete Rose realizes the enormity of his record. "I never have and never will say I'm a better player than Cobb or the best player who ever lived. But no one can ever deny that no man that ever lived has more hits than Pete Rose. I'm proud of that."

Yastrzemski's last day in Boston and now this. Pete Rose has a special quality about him and if he'd gotten the hit off me, I guess it would have been a big deal for me, too. Anytime you get 70 reporters in your face asking you how you feel about something, I guess it's a big deal."

Top of the ninth. Eddie Milner fouls off two bunts before singling. Pete Rose has another shot at history. This time against Cubs' stopper Lee Smith. He fakes a bunt at ball one. The second pitch is high and away. The count is 2-0, a perfect hitting situation. Rose takes a strike before fouling off the fourth delivery. With an even count, Rose swings mightily and strikes out.

The barrel-chested Rose (facing page) has rightfully earned the nickname Charlie Hustle, while teammate Dave Parker (above) pleaded with Rose to break the hit record at Riverfront Stadium.

The record will have to be broken in Cincinnati.

September 10, 1985: in Cincinnati, practically the whole world is waiting for Rose to break the record. The start of the game is held up 16 minutes because traffic coming to the park is so heavy. The Goodyear Blimp hovers overhead flashing "Go, Pete." NBC-TV breaks into its regularly scheduled programming

THE YEAR OF THE MILESTONE

Even if Pete Rose never broke Ty Cobb's record of 4191 hits in career, 1985 will be remembered as the year of the milestone. Three players placed their names in the history books and solidified their qualifications for entrance into Cooperstown's Hall of Fame.

Tom Seaver and Phil Niekro joined the 16 others in the 300 victory club and Rod Carew, baseball's quintessential hitter, chalked up his 3,000 career hit.

Arguably the most emotional milestone accomplished (excluding Rose, of course) was Seaver's 300th win. It was not just winning his 300th game, a feat only 16 other pitchers achieved before him. It was coming back to New York. It was returning to the city where Tom Seaver became a legend and the greatest pitcher of his era. It was coming home to do it, to the town where Tom Seaver acquired the monicker "The Franchise."

"He pitched most of his career with mediocre clubs," remarked Sparky Anderson, who once managed Seaver during the lean years in Cincinnati. "Imagine what he could have done, what his record could have been, if he'd been on some teams in their great eras like Cincinnati, Los Angeles, Pittsburgh."

In 1967 Tom Seaver joined the Mets, a team of losers, a team laughed at by the baseball fraternity for its ineptness. But two years after winning the Rookie-of-the-Year award, Seaver turned the Mets into the Miracle Mets, the 1969 World Champion Mets. That championship year brought Seaver the first of his three Cy Young awards. A year later he orchestrated a 19-strikeout masterpiece against San Diego and in 1973 his 2.08 e.r.a led the league and pushed the Mets into the World Series again. He was reknowned as the top pitcher in the majors, a class act and the Mets' link to success.

But there were low points as well. A contract dispute in 1977 led former Mets Board Chairman M. Donald Grant to swap Seaver to a rebuilding Cincinnati team on the eve of the trading deadline for four mediocre players. That was the first time Seaver was driven out of New York.

Chicago White Sox catcher Carlton Fisk (above) was fortunate to catch Tom Seaver's 300th victory. Seaver (facing page) still looks strange in a White Sox uniform.

The second time was the winter of '84. After reacquiring Seaver from the Reds, Mets general manager Frank Cashen mistakenly left Seaver unprotected in the waiver draft and Chicago quickly scooped up the crafty veteran.

"We didn't take him at the time just because he was Tom Seaver," said former White Sox g.m. Roland Hemond. "We had scouted him in 1983 and we knew we were getting a starting pitcher."

Indeed. And on August 4 Seaver walked into Yankee Stadium wearing the crest of the Sox on his chest, looking for victory number 300. The uniform looked strange and, for Seaver, it even felt strange.

"Chicago's not home for me, certainly not. I feel at home with the people I work with here. It's as good a group of guys as I've ever been with. And the city's fine. Chicago is a great city, but as far as living here, I feel like a visitor."

But as a visitor in Yankee Stadium, Seaver felt at home. The stands were packed with 54,032 fans, many Mets fans, many Yankees fans but all cheering for The Franchise. "I have some very good memories of New York and its fans," Seaver said. "Will I always think of myself as a Met? I'm not sure. Funny, when I first came up, I thought I'd never last this long to be identified with any team. But I still can pitch well, and that's important. I don't feel old. I still get satisfaction from pitching and winning."

There's no doubt Seaver derived much satisfaction from his 300th victory. It was a typical Seaver outing. Over nine innings he scattered six hits, walked one and struck out seven. Though in trouble in the eighth and ninth innings, Seaver's guile and changing speeds, a trademark in the latter stages of his career, kept the Yankees at bay.

"He's a master of changing speeds, running the ball, cutting the ball, jumping the ball," said White Sox catcher Carlton Fisk, the first to congratulate Seaver after leftfielder Reid Nichols squeezed the final out. "He has a sense of what to do and when to do it. It's almost like he is reading the batter's mind. There aren't many pitchers who have that feel, that sense. Really, when the game gets the toughest, that's when he's at his best.

"He uses everything. Every pitch is different. He has a fastball, but he may throw it at five different speeds, so it's really five different pitches.

"There aren't enough adjectives to describe him as a pitcher, person or competitor," Fisk adds. "People have been trying to dig them up for a long time, but the best one came when he first started pitching: Tom Terrific. He is terrific."

"I'm not throwing as fast as I once did," said Seaver, "but I have a better understanding of the mechanics of pitching. I've really been lucky in that I've worked with three of the best catchers of my era: Jerry Grote, Johnny Bench and now Pudge (Fisk). All of them quickly came to an understanding of what I like and how I pitch. That's extremely important. In each case, our minds started to work as one."

And for the teams Seaver played for, that meant victory. At least 300 of them.

***

Consider this. If Rod Carew doesn't get a hit in his next 700 major league at bats, his lifetime batting average will still be .300. That's how overwhelming the Panamanian-born star's hitting accomplishments are.

But even though Carew has been baseball's best hitter of his era, and even though Carew has garnered seven batting titles, a number met or surpassed only by Ty Cobb (12), Honus Wagner (8), Rogers Hornsby (7) and Stan Musial (7), Carew has often been, for some reason or another, slighted, and not given the recognition a man of his grand achievements deserves.

And in mid-summer it was a perfect time for Carew to step to the fore. With 2,999 hits, he needed one more to enter the exclusivity of the 3,000 hit club, a club frequented by players whose post-career mailing address is Hall-of-Fame, Cooperstown, New York.

Consistency has been the hallmark of Carew's career, so on August 4th, the same date Tom Seaver finished the final chapter of his storybook career by winning his historic 300th in his old stomping ground, Carew remained consistently in the background as he quietly singled off Minnesota lefthander Frank Viola for his 3,000th base hit.

A quick flick of the wrists, a drag bunt, a lined single up the middle. Perhaps it is the relative ease with which Carew plays the game that makes people take him for granted. Perhaps it is his style, a singles hitter (he's number seven on the all-time list for singles) who works diligently at his task, that makes people forget. One thing that can't be forgotten, though, is his production.

Coming out of the Minnesota chain where heavy bombers like Harmon Killebrew and Tony Oliva resided, Carew was a cut and slash hitter. In his rookie campaign, he hit .292, enough for the American League rookie award (Tom Seaver won the National League honors, of course). After batting just .273 his sophomore season, Carew went on a tear that saw him win seven batting titles, hit over .300 and terrorize pitchers the next 16 years.

"He can hit a ball within a yard whenever he wants," commented former pitcher Stan Williams. "The only other one I ever saw able to do that was Stan Musial."

"You can't pitch him one certain way," said future Hall-of-Famer Nolan Ryan. "There's no one pitch that gets him out consistently. He'd kill you if you tried to pitch a certain pattern."

Perhaps that's what American League

pitchers attempted to do in 1977, when Carew nearly became the first player since Ted Williams to hit .400 or better in a season. After hovering around the .400 mark, Carew "settled" for a .388 average.

"Ever since I was six or seven years old I could always swing the bat," Carew said. "It never came hard to me, but I've learned more about hitting – the fine points."

And how. That's how Carew found himself in a position to achieve his 3,000 hit on August 4th. With one out, Carew blooped a single to the opposite field,

Above: Reggie Jackson and Rod Carew talk it over. Carew (facing page), a student of the game, studies the opposition.

another Carew trademark, to take his place in history. Catcher Bob Boone hugged him, manager Gene Mauch helped him remove the historic first base bag and 41,630 stood to give him their unwavering applause.

"Rod was born with great hand-eye coordination, but he worked his rear end off to become a great hitter," said Mauch. "He has 3,000 hits and he's gotten 100 in practice for every one of those because he's practiced more than anyone you ever saw."

"I'm glad it's over," said a relieved Carew after the hit. "Now I can sleep at night."

Why not? It's the pitchers that face him who usually have trouble sleeping at night.

***

Success has not come quickly for Phil Niekro. Throughout his entire 21-year baseball career, the knuckleballing specialist has needed to wait before success tapped him on his talented right arm.

It took the 47-year-old Niekro five full minor league seasons before feeding his floating, fluttering knuckleballs on the major league level, and eight seasons (at the age of 25) until he became firmly ensconsed in the Atlanta Braves rotation. And although he participated in two league championship series and two All-Star games, Niekro has yet to play in a World Series, a dream he'll have to wait a little longer for.

So it's no wonder that Niekro labored until the final day of the 1985 baseball season in search of his 300th victory, a

milestone only 17 others have accomplished. In fact, it took Niekro 27 days and four starts from the time he won number 299 until he stepped into the elite 300 win club. But the way he did it was worth the wait.

All his career, Niekro's been worth the wait. Signed as a free agent by the Milwaukee Braves organization in 1958, Niekro developed slowly, working his way through the Braves' system with stops in Wellsville, McCook, Jacksonville, Austin, Louisville and Denver. Add in a year Niekro served in the military, and you don't exactly have the glamour life he expected when he left his farm in Blaine, Ohio. But Niekro persevered, never giving up on his dream to play in the major leagues.

Finally, the Braves saw fit to give him a chance. His first full season (1965) in the

forties Niekro produced. In his two seasons in New York (at the ages of 45 and 46), he posted a 32-20 record, pitched over 200 innings each season and nearly helped the Yankees to a pennant in 1985.

Despite not winning a spot in the playoffs, Niekro topped off a vintage campaign by garnering his 300th victory after almost a month of waiting.

Following his 299th win on September 8th, Niekro suffered a few physical ailments and was hit hard the final month of the season. When he lost his third straight decision on September 25, he was reminded of Early Wynn, who also found gaining his 300th win as tough as a far-sighted man threading a needle. Wynn, who ironically also won his 299th on September 8th (1962), needed seven starts and a relief appearance before finally winning the milestone game (and also retiring immediately afterwards).

"I hadn't thought about talking to Wynn," Niekro said at the time. "I did talk to Tom Seaver earlier and he told me, 'Win it quick.' I think maybe I'll call him again and ask him how he did it. Maybe I'll ask him to teach me his fastball and slider."

Niekro didn't need a tutor. On the final day of the season he won his 300th game, an 8-0 whitewashing of the East Division Champion Toronto Blue Jays and, incredibly, he did it with a slip pitch, a curve and as he described it "a deadfish fastball." He threw only three knuckleballs all day, that to the final batter Jeff Burroughs. And, at 46 years and 188 days young, Niekro replaced Satchel Paige as the oldest pitcher in history to record a shutout.

"I wanted to prove I could win without the knuckleball," Niekro said. "But I needed a strikeout to end the game and figured, 'Why not use the pitch that got me here?' This shows you don't have to throw 95 miles an hour or have a Dwight Gooden curve to win in the big leagues. People with lesser talent should be encouraged."

But Niekro's history-making victory did not end without a few light moments. Starting the ninth, manager Billy Martin warmed three relievers in the bullpen. While Martin laughed in the dugout Phil did a double take. "I didn't expect that," Niekro said, "but knowing Billy that didn't surprise me."

And with two out in the ninth, Niekro's baby brother Joe, 40, a late-season acquisition, trotted to the mound to discuss stategy on how to pitch to the next batter. After Burroughs ended the game by flailing at a vintage Niekro knuckler, the Yankee dugout emptied and the celebration began.

For Phil Niekro, it was worth the wait.

big leagues was spent mopping up in the bullpen and after splitting the next season between Atlanta (the Braves moved their franchise to Atlanta) and Triple A Richmond, Niekro and his knuckleball found a spot in the starting rotation and stayed almost two decades.

A smart and durable pitcher, Niekro proved to be the kingpin of the Braves staff for 17 seasons (before moving to the Yankees for two years), winning 20 games three times and leading them to division titles in 1969 and 1982. And while Niekro piled up a mantle full of accolades (winner of numerous Gold Gloves, and all-star honors), his fluttering knuckleball baffled both hitters and catchers alike. Even Niekro had no idea where the ball would travel, producing a sack full of negatives.

Rod Carew (facing page) and Phil Niekro (above) are both quiet superstars. Their statistics, however, say enough for them to be considered strongly for the Hall of Fame when they retire.

Besides winning 300 games. Niekro has lost a record 230 National League contests, led the league in hit batsmen and wild pitches thrice and holds the mark for lifetime wild pitches in the N.L.

But while Niekro's knuckleball was entirely unpredictable, the man himself was totally predictable. Anyone that managed him knew he was a gamer, that every fifth day Niekro would be on the rubber. Four times he led the majors in innings pitched and even in his mid-

BASEBALL'S SUPERSTARS

"It's been Dwight all year. We're just lucky to be part of his world." – Gary Carter, after catching Dwight Gooden's record-breaking 20th victory.

One cannot tell a lot about Dwight Gooden from his expressions. Always calm, always poised, always so humble, Dwight Gooden's face is a mask of indifference on and off the field. One forgets that Dwight Gooden put the finishing touches on a Cy Young season at the age of 20, an age when such pitching maestros as Sandy Koufax and Bob Gibson were, in baseball years, still learning how to walk.

Gooden is past the walking stage. At 20 years old, with two baseball seasons behind him, Dwight Gooden appears destined to become one of the best pitchers ever to step onto the pitching rubber. His exploding 90-plus mile-per-hour fastball combined with a devastating curveball has led to many a scene of a hitter nearly screwing himself into the home plate area. Add the poise and guile of a veteran, the intense desire to succeed, and you have the makings of the finest hurler – ever.

"The kid is going to become one of the greatest of all time if he doesn't get hurt," said Montreal scout Ed Lopat. "His instincts are fantastic. He does things at 20 that it takes most pitchers 10 years in the bigs to learn.

"He has (Bob) Feller's fastball and one thing he does reminds me of Satchel Paige. It's the way he inhales the ball when the catcher throws it back, as though he can't wait to get it and pitch again."

"You can rank him anywhere," said the National League's reigning home run king Mike Schmidt. "He takes the mound with stuff as good as Gibson's ever was."

"He's 20 going 40," said Mets coach Bud Harrelson. "I'm still amazed with him, with his maturity for his age. Tom (Seaver) never had his (Gooden's) curve. Without comparing their ages, there are a lot of parallels. They were both mature, veteran-type pitchers at an early age. Doc just amazes everybody and he's such a good kid. Nothing has gone to his head and he's the talk of baseball."

Former Cardinal Joaquin Andujar is effusive in his praise for Gooden (facing page), while Davey Johnson (above) just feels secure.

And if anybody had a reason to get a big head it's Gooden. Consider the accomplishments after just two major league seasons.

* The youngest pitcher in modern baseball history to win 20 games in a season.

* In 1985, Gooden led the major leagues in wins (24), strikeouts (268), and earned run average (1.53), becoming only the seventh pitcher in baseball history to sweep the pitching Triple Crown categories.

* Had the longest winning streak (14 games from May 30 to August 25) and longest shutout streak (31 straight scoreless innings) in the majors in 1985.

* Joined Herb Score (whose strikeout record Gooden dashed in 1984) as the only pitchers in baseball history to fan more than 200 batters in both of their first two seasons.

* Showing his versatility, Gooden broke a Mets record by smacking 21 hits, the most by a New York pitcher since Tom Seaver's 18 in 1971.

* Gooden has 26 double figure strikeout games in only 66 major league starts.

The sheer numbers themselves are awesome, but even more striking is that four teams bypassed Gooden in the 1982 draft, allowing the Mets gladly to scoop him up with the fifth pick.

"He was long, loose and limber," said Mets vice president of baseball operations and the man responsible for drafting Dwight, Joe McIlvaine. "He had poise and he could throw the ball over the plate. We probably had seven or eight people look at him (in high school). You don't always see a pitcher at his best in high school because he's playing other positions when he's not pitching. But at the end of the season he was in an all-star game and he had a week's rest before he pitched. That day he threw 89-90 (m.p.h.).

"The growth potential was so evident," McIlvaine adds. "He breaks all the rules. He's up there (in majors) before he's supposed to be."

In his first full season in professional ball, Gooden struck out 300 batters in 191 innings en route to a 19-4 record at Lynchburg of the Carolina League. From there he moved to Tidewater, the Mets' Triple A affiliate, where he helped manager Dave Johnson win the Triple A World Series. And when spring training rolled around, Johnson, appointed Mets manager over the winter, urged a cautious Mets g.m. Frank Cashen that Gooden was ready for the major leagues.

And how. In his first major league start against the Houston Astros, Gooden hurled five innings, allowed one run and earned the victory. But that was just the beginning. With each passing start, the legend of Doctor K came to the fore. Batters were fanned at alarming rates as Gooden displayed the stuff that made legends out of Sandy Koufax and Bob Gibson. Soon, the Shea Stadium faithful nicknamed him Doctor K and the baseball world took to its heart this precocious 19-year-old.

Gooden became the youngest player in an all-star game and quickly showed the American League his stuff by

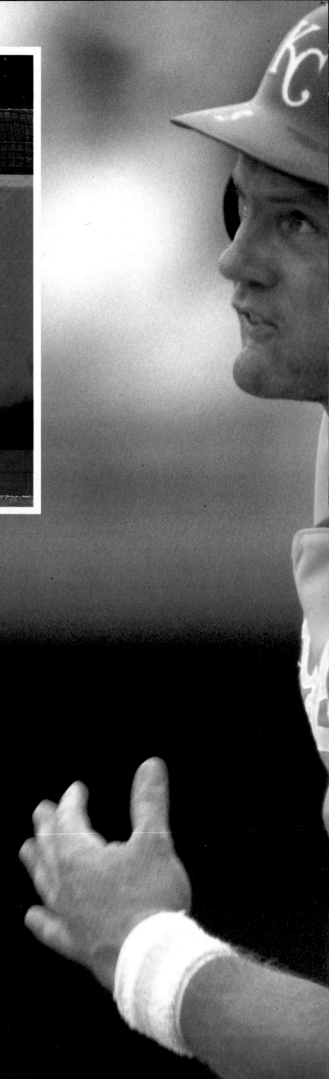

George Brett (main picture) finished second in the batting race to Wade Boggs (inset bottom left). Jim Rice (inset top left) is one of only three Red Sox ever to collect three seasons with more than 200 runs.

striking out the side in an inning of work in the All-Star game. It gets better. In September, when Gooden seemed to be hitting his stride, he tied the modern record for most strikeouts in two consecutive games by fanning 32. He broke Herb Score's rookie strikeout record (276) and averaged more strikeouts per inning (11.39) than any pitcher in baseball history. Of course, he won the Rookie-of-the-Year honors.

"One thing I like about Gooden is that he takes everything in stride," said former St. Louis hurler Joaquin Andujar, who does exactly the opposite. "It doesn't seem like anything fazes him. A bad call by the umpire, or he makes a bad pitch, he just goes out and throws the next pitch. He doesn't let anything bother him. There are a whole lot of guys here who have had great arms and who should have done this and should have done that. But they just had a hard time getting disciplined with their attitude."

Gooden's attitude is clearly an important ingredient to his prowess. Despite all the success, despite all the achievements, Gooden still found flaws in his game. In 1984, runners stole an alarming 47 of 50 attempts off him. So in the winter instructional league, Gooden worked on quickening his delivery and picked off a number of baserunners in 1985. He also developed a changeup and refined his curveball. He even changed his philosophy and that meant more problems for the hitters.

"I realized halfway through last season (1984) that I couldn't go out there and say, 'Here comes the curve or here comes the fastball,'" Gooden said. "The more you pitch, the more your learn. I feel more comfortable going after locations this year than I did before."

The location many batters found themselves heading for after a bout with Gooden was the bench. While Gooden was, uh, good, his rookie season, he proved to be majestic his second campaign. A second all-star selection and going almost four months without a defeat, Gooden posted a 24-4 record, a microscopic 1.53 e.r.a. Naturally, he became the youngest pitcher to win the Cy Young award (by unanimous decision, no less) and naturally, he took it with the same grace, the same indifference with which he mows down opposing hitters.

"This surprises me a great bit," he said at the news conference announcing the award. "Last year, I didn't even think I'd make the team. Growing up, I didn't think about Cy Young. I just wanted to make the major leagues. And I figured even if I did I'd just be an average pitcher, an average ballplayer."

Somehow, it didn't work out that way. Just ask National League batters.

When a player is branded a label, it usually sticks. It was four years after he graduated high school. It was following three successive .300 or better minor league campaigns. But still, the label stuck, like an illegal parking sticker does to the windshield of a car. Tough like an adhesive, the label Wade Boggs wore did not suit him well. Good singles hitter, no power, can't field.

"I got a label on me that not only didn't I have enough power," said Boggs,

"but that I couldn't play third base defensively. Everyone had read the label 'Can't field,' and decided I was just another Triple A player."

It's something Boggs has had to fight since being selected by the Boston Red Sox in the seventh round of the 1976 June draft. Even his first major league manager, Ralph Houk, remembers Boggs having to dispel the albatross hanging around his neck.

"Everyone told me he could hit major league pitching, but I heard that he'd probably have to be a first baseman or a DH. Then I played him at third in spring training just to see what he'd look like and he didn't look bad. A lot better than what I thought."

Wade Boggs has been impressing others since stepping into the starting lineup on June 25, 1982 after Carney Lansford went down in a home plate collision with Detroit's Lance Parrish. He finished the 1982 season with a .349 batting average, but failed to qualify for the batting title because he didn't bat the required number of times. And in that short half season of playing regular, Boggs repudiated the "no field" charges by making only eight errors.

Willie McGee (above) and Wade Boggs (facing page) were batting champions in the National and American Leagues.

"I've listened to what people have said I had to do to make the big leagues," said Boggs. "When they told me I had to hit for more power, I worked on it, went out and hit 41 doubles (in Pawtucket). When they told me I couldn't play defense, I asked them why, got the answer on my shortcomings and worked on them.

"The first thing I did was learn to dive for balls by playing pepper for a half-hour at a time and having someone alternate hitting balls to either side of me. They told

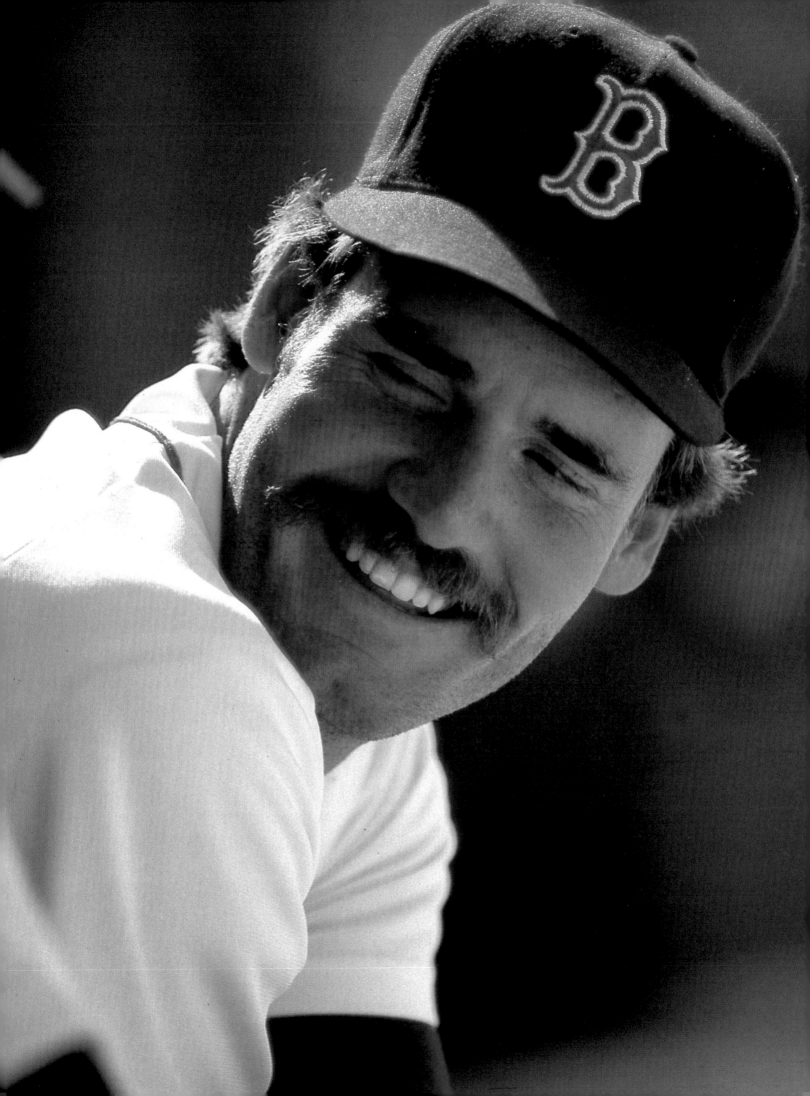

me I didn't have a strong enough arm, so I set out to improve that by throwing and throwing and throwing – long toss, short toss, you name it. They told me my hands were bad, so I took as many grounders as I could."

But the topic all baseball people talk about when the subject is Wade Boggs is hitting. In his four seasons in the major leagues, Boggs' career average is .351. In a list of lifetime batting leaders after four seasons, Boggs ranks number seven of all-time, ahead of Stan Musial, Honus Wagner and Lloyd Waner. Boggs is the only player to crack the top 25 after four years since World War II. He is the new Rod Carew and Pete Rose rolled into one. The sweet swing of Carew, the determination and work ethic of Rose.

"Number one," said Boston hitting coach Walt Hriniak, "he's got a balanced, workable stance. Number two, he's got a disciplined strike zone. He's not afraid of taking pitches. But the most important thing that makes him such a great hitter is that he lowers his head and sees the baseball better than anyone I've ever seen. Mentally, he's a very dedicated hitter. He's constantly working at his trade. He's always looking for ways to improve himself. He not only wants to be a good hitter, he wants to be a great hitter. In my opinion, his ability to get a base hit is the best I've ever seen."

"I've always felt I could hit any pitcher at any time," opines Boggs. "Since no two

When the Yankees signed Dave Winfield (left) to a free agent contract, Willie McGee (above) was sent to the Cards to make room on the roster. Bret Saberhagen (facing page) won the A.L. Cy Young Award in 1985.

pitchers work alike, it doesn't make sense to hit the same way. That's why I shift a lot at the plate, sometimes between pitches. But it's so subtle that no one notices but me."

Boggs' hitting mechanisms may be subtle, but the end results have pitchers seeking a method to stop him. After his successful 1982 campaign, Boggs continued his progress by hitting .361, and banging out 210 hits to win the batting title going away in 1983. By his standards, he faltered in 1984, hitting "only" .325 and knocking in 55 runs. The falloff in production led to speculation that Boggs would be dealt.

Luckily for Boston, they held on to Boggs and he came through with one of the most spectacular hitting displays in decades. In winning his second batting title in four years, Boggs hit .363, rapped 240 hits, breaking Hall-of-Famer Tris Speaker's club mark of 223 in 1912. He became one of only three Red Sox to collect 200 or more hits three times (Johnny Pesky and Jim Rice) and his 187 singles smashed Willie Wilson's American League record of 184. Finally, he tied Chuck Klein's major league mark by reaching safety in 135 games. All as a lefthanded hitter in Boston's Fenway Park.

Washington, Cardinals third base coach Chuck Hiller is frantically waving McGee on for a certain inside-the-park home run. But the kid with sprinter's speed cruises into third and shuts down all engines. A triple it will be.

McGee and his teammates can laugh about it later. After all, the Cards won the game handily and even a manager can forgive rookie mistakes.

"I never saw anything like it," said Cards manager Whitey Herzog. "He

Besides leading the league in batting, McGee also helped the Cardinals into the World Series and ultimately was named the National League's Most Valuable Player.

"It's an award that shows I put everything together," said the modest centerfielder. "I'm very pleased. I felt I had a good season; I felt I did my job. I'm satisfied. I progressed a lot faster than I thought I would. I feel I'm still young and still have some things to learn. But it has

Wade Boggs can say he erased that dreadful label that had been haunting him his entire career. Now the only label that's hanging around his neck is that of batting champion.
***
It's October of 1982 and Cardinals rookie Willie McGee is at the plate in the first game of the league championship series. In the third inning of a scoreless game, McGee opens the frame by bouncing a grounder past the first baseman and down the rightfield line. A player of ordinary speed would have a standup double, easy. But with McGee running the bases, the St. Louis dugout is screaming triple.

As the ball rattles around the rightfield corner in Busch Memorial Stadium and skips past Atlanta's Claudell

could've had five bases and he got three."

"He could have had six bases on that ball," remarked former teammate Bruce Sutter at the time. "He could've kept going and ended up at second. That's all talent you see out there. Just raw talent. When the kid learns what the game's all about, he's going to be a superstar."

Not only is Bruce Sutter an outstanding relief pitcher, but the Atlanta Braves stopper is quite a prophet. Three years after breaking in as a crude talent, McGee smoothed the rough edges of his game and turned in one of the most remarkable seasons in recent memory.

The fleet switch-hitter stood the National League on its collective ear by winning the batting title with a .353 average. McGee's average represents the highest for a switch-hitter in decades.

been a special season for me. I came into the season hoping to improve my batting right-handed and be more disciplined at the plate. I'd rather be known as an all-around player able to help my team in different ways."

Just because McGee hit .353, don't get the idea he's a uni-dimensional player. Before the 27-year-old refined his hitting to become one of the league's best, he made all the plays in centerfield. And at Busch Stadium, with its artificial turf, high bounces and huge expanse, McGee's 78 rpm game transforms opponents' doubles into harmless singles. As Whitey Herzog likes to say, "McGee plays the best center field in baseball."

Herzog must look to the heavens for thanks every time McGee turns a sure gapper into an out and delivers a game-winning single. After all, it was a quirk of fate that McGee ended up in a St. Louis uniform.

During the 1981 World Series, the Yankees dealt McGee for Bob Sykes, a lefthanded pitcher since retired. Although McGee batted .322 at the Double A level, the Yankees had taken him off the minor league roster when they signed free agent Dave Winfield. Instead of losing McGee in the December draft of unprotected players, the Yankees traded him to St. Louis.

"I picked up the paper one day and read about it in the transactions," remembers McGee. "I was happy to get out of the Yankee organization to be honest with you."

"Willie Calvino, our Latin scout, had him in Mexico," Herzog said at the time. "He liked him very much. I remember Willie saying, 'He's got a chance to be better than David Green.' I said, 'If he's that good, we'd better get him.'"

Not everything has been as easy as this past season for McGee. Sure he's starred in the World Series, made the all-star team twice and has won the Gold Glove the last four years. But early in 1984, McGee suffered through a prolonged slump, the first of his career. And, like all thoroughbreds, McGee rebounded to hit .291.

"I was proud of the fact that I didn't give up," he said. "I was used to being successful, but a lot of people stuck with me and worked with me. I kept a positive attitude, and that was the hardest thing to do. "It definitely made me a better man and a better ballplayer. It made me grow up a little bit."

There's no denying McGee grew up. He possesses the National League's Most Valuable Player trophy as evidence.

***

Consider the travels and travails of one Bret Saberhagen in the past three years.

In June, 1982, the 18-year-old Saberhagen is chosen by the Kansas City Royals in the 19th round of the amateur draft. Later that month, Saberhagen concludes his career at Cleveland High School by tossing a no-hitter in a 13-0 victory over Palisades in the city championship game in Dodger Stadium. Only a first-inning error prevents Saberhagen from registering a perfect game.

In March 1983, Saberhagen begins his professional career with Fort Myers of the Florida State League. After compiling an impressive 10-5 record with a 2.30 earned run average, Saberhagen is moved to Jacksonville of the Southern League. Different league, same results. This time, the 19-year-old reaffirms his credentials and becomes the hottest prospect in the Royals organization by winning six of eight decisions while allowing less than three earned runs per game.

Spring Training, 1984, and Saberhagen wins a spot on the Kansas City pitching staff. A week before his 20th birthday, Saberhagen enters a big league game to become the youngest Kansas City Royal ever.

In December, 1984, Saberhagen weds his high school sweetheart, Janeane, after compiling a 10-11 record with a very respectable 3.48 e.r.a. Not bad for a kid that looks like he belongs more on the Howdy Doody show than This Week in Baseball.

Early October, 1985. Bret Saberhagen finishes a marvelous season with a 20-6 record, a 2.90 e.r.a., leads the Royals to the American League West title and undoubtedly becomes the kingpin of the Kansas City pitching staff.

Mid October, 1985. Bret Saberhagen is playing in the World Series against the St. Louis Cardinals. With the Royals down 2-0 in games, it's up to Saberhagen to quell the Cards and give the Royals a chance for a comeback. With the nod, Saberhagen becomes the youngest pitcher to start a World Series contest since Jim Palmer worked for Baltimore in 1966. Naturally, Saberhagen comes through with a gem, allowing only one run and cutting the Cardinals' lead in half. But that's not even the exciting part of the month for Saberhagen.

A few days later, his wife gives birth to a boy and one day after, Saberhagen finds himself on the mound in the seventh game of the World Series against ace lefthander John Tudor. No problem. While Tudor is belted, Saberhagen neatly cuts down the Cards as the Royals win their first World Series ever. Saberhagen, of course, is voted M.V.P. of the Series.

Mid November, and Saberhagen receives the final crowning glory to a superb season. In a landslide, he is named American League Cy Young Award winner. It's been quite a trio of years for Bret Saberhagen.

"I just kind of take things one day at a time," said the seemingly unaffected Saberhagen. "It's been happening fast, but I've kind of put it in perspective. I've been able to enjoy each thing that's happened to me. Some of my friends came out to see me play and said, 'Hey, you're a superstar now.' And I said, 'But I don't feel like a superstar.' I'm the same old Bret Saberhagen that I was in high school. I really don't feel like I've changed that much. I don't know... it's really strange being labeled a star. It's something I guess I'll have to live with."

And it was something Cards manager Whitey Herzog had to live with during the World Series. "He just threw strikes. He compares with Dwight Gooden, whom I consider an overpowering guy."

"He doesn't have a real weakness," said Royals manager Dick Howser. "He fields his position well, he holds runners, he doesn't walk hitters. Look at his strikeouts vs. walks. It's probably the best in the American League. You put those kinds of numbers together, why shouldn't he be a good pitcher?"

But if Saberhagen is so highly regarded now, why did over 400 players get selected before him in the amateur draft?

"The fact that he was a 19th-round draft choice is a little bit misleading, because he was a fine player during his junior year," said Kansas City general manager John Schuerholz. "Then he hurt his arm. The scout that recommended him had seen him as a junior, and he really stuck with him. He's a remarkable young man. He's got great make-up, he's got great composure, he's got great competitive spirit, and he's also blessed with a lot of ability. That's an awfully rare combination for somebody who's 21 years old."

Despite the ego-busting of being drafted in the 19th round, Saberhagen was probably better off. It allowed him to enter the minor leagues without fanfare and ultimately, his talent got him recognized.

"We made a decision after '83 that our starting pitching was not strong enough for us to be a contender," Howser said. "We had to do something about it, and you have to try your own people first. That's the organization's philosophy and I like it. Why not give them a chance? They've all been able to handle it, Saberhagen better than any of them because he has that poise and maturity you look for."

Thus, the travels of Bret Saberhagen end in Kansas City, with a World Series ring, an M.V.P. trophy and a Cy Young award to boot.

***

Picture this, and you'll have a good picture of the character of George Brett, baseball's best hitter.

Game Five of the World Series. The Royals lead St. Louis 5-1. A high foul pop is lifted towards the Kansas City Royals dugout. George Brett, the third baseman, is steaming toward it like a bulldog chasing a piece of raw meat. He glances toward the dugout. Its a five-foot drop from field level to the hard, concrete floor.

Martinez). They were out there at three o'clock every day taking batting practice with Charlie. When I finally got to .240, he said I could hit .250. And that's the way we took everything. I never thought of myself as any more than a utility infielder. In high school, I tried to be a Yaz (Carl Yastrzemski) type of hitter, you know, bat held high and way back, but I wasn't."

A look at Brett's batting stance and it's easy to tell he was a pupil of Lau's. Slightly closed and off the plate, Brett is a picture of balance, keeping his head completely still as he follows through effortlessly. With the bat back on his shoulder, Lau forced Brett to concentrate on hitting the ball over second base.

"All of a sudden I started to hit," Brett said.

And he hasn't stopped since.

Brett won the batting title in 1976 with a .333 average, but he came into national prominence in 1980 when he nearly became the first hitter since Ted Williams to bat .400. It was a monster year for Brett, and not only in batting average. He drove in 118 runs in 117 games, making him the first player since Watt Drogo to average at least one RBI per game. His slugging percentage of .664 was the highest since Mickey Mantle's .687 in 1961. His on-base

George Brett is not a unidimensional player, proven by his fine fielding at third base (above left). Brett (above) was a much happier player in 1985, avoiding the injury bug. Wade Boggs (facing page), Brett's close friend, topped him for the batting crown.

No matter. The pace quickens. A few feet from dugout, Brett goes into a full slide. Like a baserunner steaming towards home plate with the winning run, George Brett goes barreling into the dugout – feet first – in an attempt to catch the ball. But the only thing that is caught is Brett himself as Royals coach Lee May tenderly cradles the major league's best player to safety.

Such is George Brett, the baseball player. Always hustling, always working and always hitting. From his rookie season, when he hit a career-low .282, to his magical .390 season in 1980, to last season's all-around excellence, George Brett is considered by many to be baseball's quintessential hitter.

But Brett, hitter extraordinaire, was not always baseball's toughest out. In fact, Brett struggled early in his career and actually never batted over .300 until he landed in the majors. His minor league batting average? A very mortal .280.

Brett was lucky, though, because when he made it to the Royals in 1974, Charlie Lau, now deceased, was the batting instructor. Although an average player in his career, Lau was an ardent student of hitting. He took Brett under his wing and carefully guided his progress.

"After the first two months of the season I was hitting about .200," Brett said. "Charlie told me that once I got to .199, he'd step in. I saw what he was doing for others (Hal McRae and Buck

percentage led both leagues and he struck out a mere 22 times all season.

At the All-Star break Brett was batting a lukewarm .337 before getting white-hot. The second half he batted .421, hit in 30 straight games and as late as September 19 he was above the magic .400 mark. He fell off in the final two weeks of the season and had to settle for a .390 average.

"We all come here with talent," explained Brett's teammate Hal McRae about George's remarkable season. "But the stars are the ones who don't have to work at concentrating. The superstars are the ones who are unconscious. They're in a trance. That's what George was in."

Brett wasn't in it long, though. The pressure and media exposure began to wear on the All-Star third-baseman. The following year he batted .314 but missed a slew of games because of injuries. In fact the next three seasons, Brett missed a total of 115 contests and his average fell to .284 in 1984. At the age of 31, critics were saying Brett was fat, out-of-shape and injury-prone. Clearly, they said, he was on the downside of his career.

That's when Brett decided to re-dedicate himself. Over the winter of '84 he hired a trainer who put him through a rigorous workout program and a strict diet. When spring training rolled around, a new, superbly conditioned George Brett arrived. And it showed on the playing field.

Brett placed second in the American League batting race with a .335 average. He hit a career-high 30 home runs while knocking in 112 runs. He was so prolific that A.L. pitchers walked him 31 times intentionally, just two less than Ted Williams' American League record. And he played in 155 games, a most satisfying figure for Brett and his manager Dick Howser. "He told me coming into spring training this year that his goal was to play in 160 games," Howser said. "I said, 'George, I'd be satisfied with, say 150. That would be plenty good enough.'"

"I think the reason I had a good year is because I've been able to stay in the lineup," Brett said late in the season. "And if it's because of the conditioning program I went on last year, it makes it all worthwhile. I missed too many games the last three, four years and I thought it was about time that if I got in a little bit of shape, I could probably play healthier and play in more games."

And thus, terrorize American League pitchers that much more.

***

Don Mattingly is a traditionalist, so it comes as no surprise that he is upholding a tradition that began in 1923. More than 60 years ago, one Babe Ruth stood head and shoulders above other talented baseball players. Four years later, the tradition continued, this time with Lou Gehrig. As years passed, luminaries such as DiMaggio, Gordon, Rizzuto, Berra, Mantle, Maris, Howard and Munson successfully held the distinction of being the American League's Most Valuable Player.

And in a day when George Steinbrenner's outbursts hold the headlines, when being a Yankee means being the highest paid, Don Mattingly makes Yankee fans feel lucky they root for the guys in the pinstripes. Because in three major league seasons, Don Mattingly has brought back the ghosts of Ruth and Gehrig, of Maris and Munson and kept them alongside him.

Consider his first two full seasons and compare them to the first couple of seasons of present and future Hall-of-Famers. His lifetime batting average is .333, or 62 points higher than Pete Rose. His 58 home runs are 18 more than Hank Aaron, 14 more than Mickey Mantle. His 255 runs batted in are a hundred more than Stan Musial, 63 more than Reggie Jackson. It's not hard to conjure up the images of the famed Murderers' Row when Don Mattingly's name is mentioned.

His 1985 MVP season could do it all by itself. Consider the following statistical achievements. Mattingly led the majors in RBI with 145, and doubles with 48. He led the American League with 370 total bases, 21-game-winning hits, and 86 extra base hits. He was second in the A.L. in hits (211), and slugging percentage (.567), third in batting average (.324), fourth in home runs (35). He also led the A.L. firstbasemen in fielding percentage (.995), held a string of 153 errorless games and won the Gold Glove.

His 145 ribbies were the most by a Yankee since Joe DiMaggio had 155 in

George Brett gives it his all, whether on the basepaths (facing page), or just warming up (left). Don Mattingly's swing (above) produced 145 R.B.I.

1948, and he reached the 100 RBI plateau earlier than any Yankee since 1961. He became the first Yankee to collect 200-plus hits in consecutive seasons since DiMaggio did it in 1936-37 and he is the first American Leaguer to lead the majors in doubles consecutive seasons since Tris Speaker in 1920-23.

Now consider that Mattingly accomplished all that despite a rather slow start in 1985. Before spring training began, the 24-year-old suffered knee cartilage damage working out with weights. He underwent arthroscopic surgery and missed the first 18 Grapefruit

League contests. And in grand fashion, he made a spectacular spring debut, clouting a home run in his first spring at-bat.

But things were not all smiles for Mattingly. A run-in with Steinbrenner over a salary dispute pushed the usually mild-mannered Mattingly to utter, "I won't forget this when next year comes around. George didn't want to take care

lefthanders," he said. "I should do better than. And I don't walk enough, so I could be a little more patient and get better pitches to hit. You can always improve."

And he's been improving ever since the Yankees made him a 19th round draft choice in 1979. Mattingly began his professional career at Oneonta of the New York Penn League and quickly stamped himself a prospect by hitting

booed or hassled. His attitude is, 'Treat us all the same.' You don't see that in a lot of young players."

You also don't see many young players win batting titles. Usually it takes a player several years to become comfortable in the league, to learn the pitchers and to become patient at the plate. It took Pete Rose six seasons before he won his first batting title, Rod Carew three. Mattingly, in his first full campaign, nosed teammate Dave Winfield on the final day of the season to win the batting crown at .344.

"He sees into a pitcher just about as well as any young player I've ever seen," said Lou Piniella, the former hitting instructor turned manager, when

Ted Turner and Yanks' owner George Steinbrenner share a laugh (above), but Don Mattingly (left) had the last laugh on George after signing a $1.4 million contract. George Brett (facing page) scrambles into the bag safely against Toronto.

Mattingly was brought up. "In that sense, he's already like a veteran in the way he thinks. He's always up there with a real good idea of what a pitcher is trying to do to him. You put that together with his quick stroke and his keen eye – the ball always looks like a grapefruit to him – and you see why he's a sure .300 hitter or better."

"Hitters like (Wade) Boggs and Rod Carew seem impossible to pitch to," said former Toronto manager Bobby Cox, "but Mattingly is almost tougher because he'll drive the ball for the RBI, given that situation. Pitch him away and he'll pull the slider right inside first base to get runs in. There are a lot of great players in the Yankees' lineup, but Mattingly is the one everyone worries about."

But that's to be expected. After all, he's got a tradition to uphold.

of me, so I'll take care of myself from now on. They may have to hold me back because I may be playing too hard now."

It appeared Mattingly was pressing, for he didn't hit his first home run until May and his average tailed to .285 in mid-June before the talent took over. Following an oh for 19 skein, Mattingly went on hitting streaks of 20 and 19 games en route to a .390 August batting average. And despite finishing the season with a .324 average, Mattingly saw ways to improve. "I hit under .300 against

.349. Stops at Greensboro, Nashville and Columbus followed, with a .300 or better average at each locale. Finally, in June of '83, Mattingly was a major leaguer to stay, hitting .283 in the 91 games he played in.

"You see a lot of people with great talent," said former teammate Steve Kemp. "Great talent and desire like Donnie's can turn a player into a superstar.

"Donnie's not caught up in what he's doing. He cares about his teammates; he doesn't like to see his teammates get

A BUMPER CROP

"He's one of those guys who creates excitement. He has a certain air, a certain electricity about him." – Cardinals manager Whitey Herzog about rookie sensation Vince Coleman.

The situation: Wrigley Field, Chicago. Rookie flash Vince Coleman is on second base, equally swift Willie McGee on first. The Cubs' pitcher looks back toward second twice, maybe three times, trying to keep the mercurial Coleman close. Shortstop Larry Bowa is dashing from side to side between his regular position and the second bag, also hoping that the Redbird remains perched in the neighborhood of second base.

The pitcher comes to the belt and delivers. With the leg kick toward home, Coleman and McGee take off on the double steal. Coleman's legs and arms churn into a blur of motion as catcher Jody Davis slingshots the ball to third base. It's late. Stolen base. But the fleet rookie overslides the base. Now, he's in a rundown.

Wiggling back and forth between third base and home plate, Coleman looks like he's playing an inside-out game of monkey-in-the-middle with Ron Cey and Davis. Incredibly, Coleman forces a poor throw, and streaks home with an easy run. McGee winds up at third. It's a double-double steal.

This was a microcosm of the 1985 season for one Vincent Maurice Coleman, a.k.a. The Man of Steal. He was the sparkplug for the St. Louis engine, the man who set the merry-go-round of runs in motion. He's the man whose 110 swipes shattered the rookie stolen base record of 72, set just one year prior by Philadelphia's Juan Samuel. Simply, he's the man who made the Redbirds run.

"Vince not only distracts the pitchers and forces them to throw more fastballs," said one of the main beneficiaries of Coleman's speed, Tommy Herr, "but he gets the infielders jockeying around out there, which opens up holes. It's hard to overestimate his value to us."

Perhaps the Cardinals found out how important the presence of the National League's Rookie-of-the-Year was to the offense when the strange case of the tarpaulin transpired in the league championship series. By some accident, Busch Stadium's automatic tarpaulin

St. Louis Cardinals rookie leftfielder Vince Coleman (facing page) took the baseball world by storm after his recall in May, stealing 110 bases and shattering Juan Samuel's (above) rookie record of 72.

rolled out prior to Game Four and pinned an unsuspecting Coleman to the artificial turf. The tarp lay atop Coleman several minutes before it could be removed, and the weight injured Coleman's most precious possession – his legs. Without the stolen base king, the Cards' offense faltered badly in the World Series.

But if not for a quirk of fate, Coleman may never have even seen the big leagues in 1985. With the St. Louis outfield stocked with studs like Willie McGee, Lonnie Smith and Andy Van Slyke, Coleman had no chance to break into the starting lineup. The Cards braintrust didn't want Coleman to sit on the bench when he could be playing full-time in Triple A at Louisville. But injuries to McGee (no wonder he was M.V.P.) and reserve outfielder Tito Landrum forced Whitey Herzog to recall Coleman in May.

"I needed a body, and we'll give him a taste of the major leagues," said Herzog at the time of the recall. "It might be two days, it might be six days or it might be never. You never know." "I knew when I got the chance I wanted to play the best of my ability," said Coleman. "I wanted to let my ability take over."

His ability to steal bases has never been questioned by anyone in the Cardinals' organization. Coleman was the Cardinals' 10th round selection in the June 1982 draft out of Florida A & M, where he played football and proved to be one of the best punters in the nation. Instead, he opted for baseball and in his first full professional season in 1983 at Macon of the South Atlantic League, Coleman set a professional baseball record by stealing 145 bases in just 113 games. Even more astounding is that he missed 31 games with a broken hand.

He was promoted all the way to Louisville of the American Association in 1984 and though struggling with the bat – he hit .257 in only his second season of switch-hitting – he finished with 101 stolen bases. His stolen base prowess and disturbing effect on pitchers in the minors had managers shaking their heads. "All he has to do is make contact with the ball," said one minor-league manager. "He's so fast, he makes a routine groundout close at first. He makes your infielders nervous because if he gets on first, you know he's going to second. If you make an error, he'll be on third or home. My pitchers start worrying about Coleman back at the motel."

Coleman has been timed at 3.7 from home to first base. The average player covers the 90-foot distance in 4.2. That is one of the reasons Coleman became only the fourth major-leaguer to steal over 100 bases in a season. The others? Rickey Henderson, Lou Brock and Maury Wills. Select company, to say the least.

"All of the attention has surprised me a little bit," Coleman said. "I'm not really trying to establish a name. I'm just thankful I'm in the major leagues. You have to try to establish a name in the minor leagues because you're trying to get there. I want to wake up every day with the attitude that I have to go out and play hard to maintain a job. I don't feel I'm established yet. I've learned a lot from the guys I'm around every day, and it wouldn't be smart for me not to go up and ask questions. Sometimes they come to me, and it's paid off. I don't see any reason why things can't continue to stay this way."

And for pitchers and catchers in the National League, that's a gruesome thought.
***
The tell-tale signs of stardom were apparent the first month of the 1985 baseball season. A quick glance at the record confirms this. In his first three starts of the season, Tom Browning, the Cincinnati Reds' 25-year-old rookie, won two games, hurled a combined 24 innings allowing 14 hits, and only one earned run. Any mathematician will tell you that adds to a microscopic 0.38 earned run average.

Obviously, Tom Browning did not keep that pace the rest of the season. There's not one mortal, not even Dwight Gooden, who could maintain that. But the gritty lefthander, who's been compared favorably to "Catfish" Hunter, managed to do something no rookie pitcher has accomplished in over 30 years – win 20 games. The last first-year pitcher to realize a 20-win season was Bob Grim of the Yankees in 1954.

"Out of 27 outs, he's going to have 16 or 17 fly balls," said former Reds pitching coach Jim Kaat. "He's aggressive, he goes after hitters and keeps the ball down. His fastball and control are his strengths. He's got to make his slider shorter and quicker. The screwball makes him as tough on righties as he is on lefties."

Tom Browning is not cut from the power pitcher's mold. Sure he possesses a good fastball, but that's not what wins Browning games. His superior smarts, his craftmanship, his guile are what put him in the record books. It is his cerebral approach to the game which distinguishes the Casper, Wyoming native from a rookie pitching novice.

"It's like I've been saying," said Pete Rose, Browning's manager and record-breaker himself. "These guys today don't pitch like rookies. They might be the age of rookies, but they don't pitch like rookies. Someone did a good job with him. He's always around the plate, always challenging you. He's a bulldog. He's got a lot of character, a lot of intestinal fortitude. When he gets in trouble he goes right at you."

"He doesn't have the kind of stuff where he can throw it right down the middle, but he's really smart," said Houston Astros pitcher Mike Scott. "He's two inches off the plate or paints the corners. I know you can't luck into 20 wins, that's for sure."

If someone suggested that Browning would become a star pitcher in the major leagues five years ago, the person most surprised probably would have been Tom Browning. Not that Browning ever wanted to do anything else. In fact, as he says, "You take baseball away from me, you might as well shoot me."

But despite a solid pitching career at LeMoyne College in New York, Browning wasn't drafted as a junior when players with potential and aspirations moved to the professional leagues. "It was a big blow," remembered Browning. "Nobody even looked at me. I had nothing else to do. I knew nothing but baseball."

But Browning persevered. He left school and played that summer in the Shenandoah Valley League and luckily caught the attention of a coach from Tennessee Wesleyan University who offered him a baseball scholarship. A year of fine pitching later, he found himself in Riverfront Stadium in a pre-draft tryout. He impressed the Reds' brass and was selected in the ninth round of the 1982 draft.

Following a 4-8 professional debut season, Browning developed the screwball at the Reds' Instructional League and it jettisoned him through the Cincinnati system. He compiled an 8-1 record at Tampa with a 1.49 earned run average on his way to Riverfront.

"I'm no phenom like Dwight Gooden is, or even Jay Tibbs," said Browning. "I paid my dues. I learned more about the game before I signed (a contract) than I've learned since. I don't mean just pitching, I mean my attitude about the game."

His attitude is one of all business, no nonsense. When Browning's on the mound, the foremost thing on his mind is recording outs. "He's definitely a throwback to the old-time player," said Reds coach George Scherger. "He just goes out there all business and throws and does everything he can to help you win. There is no selfishness about him, none, and that's kind of rare these days." "He is intense," said teammate Dave Parker. "He's a very intense young man, a competitor."

"When I'm pitching," Browning relates, "I feel like I have to keep things inside. Everyone talks about my poise, but watching me you can't tell. I may be burning up about something, I may be mad as hell. When I'm not playing, that's the time to yell and scream."

By the statistics, Browning didn't have much to yell and scream about in 1985. After splitting his first 18 decisions, he won 11 in a row, including the record-setting 20th victory, a typical outing where he allowed two runs in seven and a third innings.

"I was nervous as hell," said Browning about his 20th victory. "I tried to put it in the back of my mind and it still kept popping up. Every time I went out there I was more nervous."

But the only ones who are nervous now are the batters that have to face him.
***
The name Ozzie, when applied to the position of shortstop, conjures up the image of a slick infielder gliding across the diamond to produce a wondrous defensive gem. Moving gracefully to the hole, extending the glove and coddling the ball, this Nureyev in cleats balances himself and fires a strike to barely nip the baserunner. And when the name Ozzie is evoked in such a manner, the only person who comes to mind is the "Wizard of Oz"

– Ozzie Smith. Or does it?

There's another Ozzie out there who is forcing baseball people to take notice and regard defense as the best offense. Ozzie Guillen, the 21-year-old American League Rookie-of-the-Year, is following in the footsteps of the Cardinals' Smith and the last great Venezuelan Chicago White Sox shortstop, Hall-of-Famer Luis Aparicio. "Ozzie was truly the finest rookie in the American League," said his manager Tony La Russa. "He's a great young player. He did not play like a 21-year-old rookie. He played more like a seasoned veteran."

"Ozzie probably has as good instincts as any player in the game," said White Sox executive vice president of

baseball operations Ken Harrelson. You certainly don't have to tell him what to do on the baseball field. He's a thoroughbred and I'm really glad he's ours."

It is no secret why Guillen easily outdistanced the competition for rookie-of-the-year balloting. One quick look at his defensive statistics shows how valuable he was to the Sox. Playing in 150 games, the sure-handed Guillen committed just 12 errors, the fewest number of miscues by any regular shortstop in the majors. His .980 fielding percentage also topped the majors. But perhaps even more important, only one error led to an unearned run all season. It's a statistic like that which makes a pitching staff comfortable.

"In spring training, he knew me two days when he came up and told me he'd make an unassisted double play on the day I won No. 300 this year," said Tom Seaver, an admirer of Guillen's. "A rookie and he's saying that. He's terrific."

Guillen, of course, did turn an unassisted double play in Seaver's 300th win against the Yankees, making him, if nothing else, oracular. It's too bad he didn't predict that he'd knock in the winning run in the same game, a feat he calls "my biggest thrill."

Cardinals switch hitter Vince Coleman (above) set a professional baseball record by stealing 145 bases at Macon of the South Atlantic League, despite missing 31 games with a broken hand. Tom Browning (above left) emerged as the outstanding rookie pitcher, winning 20 games for the Reds.

Ozzie Guillen (main picture) proved to be the class of the A.L. rookies. Vince Coleman joined Rickey Henderson (inset top right) in the 100 plus S.B. club, while Tom Browning (inset bottom right) won 20 games for the Reds.

was approached by Ernesto Aparicio, the uncle of Luis Aparicio and the godfather-type figure in Venezuelan baseball. "Ernesto said to me, 'I want to take you to my house to live with me.' I said, 'For what?' Aparicio said, 'You be ready for a tryout.' I said, 'A tryout for what?' He said, 'For baseball,' and I said, 'I don't play baseball. I'm a volleyball player.'" Ernesto then told Guillen about the virtues of playing baseball. Most notably, the money. Guillen was sold.

"Ernesto's got like a baseball school," remembers Guillen. "He teaches boys to play. He got to be my second daddy. The first time he started to teach me, a ball hit me and I got a stitch in the mouth. I was going to quit, but Aparicio didn't let me."

And a good thing, because Guillen proved to be an instant success. He signed as a free agent with the Padres in December of 1980 and quickly moved through the organization. From Bradenton to Reno to Beaumont to Las Vegas, Guillen proved himself at every level in the field. The only question was his ability to hit major league pitching. And when the White Sox traded for him, they had no delusions of grandeur. "He far exceeded our expectations," said La Russa. "We expected him to hit about .240 and provide us some solid defense. Instead, he hits around .270 (.273 to be exact) and leads the major leagues in fielding at shortstop."

The season did not begin as cheerfully as it ended, though. Guillen found himself mired in a horrendous slump, and on June 10th hit bottom with a .210 average. The memories of minor league hitting failures were fresh, but the strong-willed Guillen refused to succumb to them. "I've had hard times in the minors," Guillen said. "I went 0-31 in Double A and 0-29 in Triple A. Here, I went 0-21 and I didn't lose my mind when I had a hard time with the bat. I told myself, 'I can handle this. I can do it.'"

"We made him aware that first of all he wasn't swinging at strikes because they weren't throwing him strikes," said Chicago batting instructor Mike Lum in mid-season. "We showed him he only had a 2-1 count on him five times all season. We got him to try to work the count in his favor."

But, as the season progressed, Guillen settled down, became more comfortable and batted .302 the rest of the way. "He's settled in the league now. He's seen all the teams and he's become more aggressive at the plate. I think it was just a matter of time before be became the Ozzie Guillen we all know he could be offensively."

And for any Ozzie who covers the infield with the grace of Nureyev, that's a bonus.

But the White Sox did not pay a king's ransom for Guillen's soothsayer abilities. In the summer of '84, former White Sox scout (and now general manager of the Chicago Bulls of the National Basketball Association) Jerry Krause touted Guillen to former Chicago general manager Roland Hemond. "Last summer Krause told me he wanted to go out and watch the top five shortstops in the minor leagues," Hemond recalled. "Jerry saw Guillen in 10 or 12 games and came back and wrote the most detailed scouting report I've ever received. It was three pages long."

It was then that Hemond negotiated a deal with the San Diego Padres, sending former American League Cy Young winner LaMarr Hoyt as one of the principals in a seven-player deal that brought Guillen to Chicago.

When scouts study Guillen's style, the first thing they notice is the

Ozzie Guillen's acrobatic glove, as well as his steady bat (facing page) brought comparisons to the Cardinals' "Wizard of Oz", Ozzie Smith (above).

---

instinctiveness with which he plays his position. The soft hands, the strong arm, those are assets anyone could have. But it's his instincts, the knack of positioning himself just right, that has scouts buzzing. And therein lies the mystery surrounding Guillen.

Guillen began his professional career in 1981 at the age of 17, but despite his intuitive nature on the diamond, Guillen insists that he didn't start playing baseball until he was 15. "I was a volleyball player and a soccer player," he said. "I lived on the beach like most volleyball players and I represented the Venezuela national team in volleyball from 12 to 16."

During one of his workouts, Guillen

THE MANAGERS

When Whitey Herzog is around, you know a trade can't be too far behind. Such is the reputation of one Dorrell Norman "Whitey" Herzog. The Cardinals' field boss is widely known in baseball circles as a master builder, a man who can turn a loser into a winner, dismantle it, and then remodel it into a winner.

And Whitey's been a winner his whole career. After a mediocre eight-year playing career, Herzog coached for the Athletics, Mets and Angels before becoming the field boss of the Texas Rangers in 1973, when his team compiled a dubious 47-91 record. Two years later, Herzog took the reins of the Kansas City Royals and began to earn his reputation.

He took one look at the artificial turf, spacious gaps and deep fences at Royals' Stadium and knew the only way to win was with speed, defense and pitching. So he gathered up all the roadrunners he could find to prowl the outfield, tossed in a powerful bat or two and relied on a solid pitching core. In 1975, Herzog guided the Royals to second place. It was the worst finish of his five-year Kansas City managerial stay. Three pennants and a "Manager of the Year" trophy followed. However, he was unable to bring home the World Championship, friction developed between Herzog and management, and ultimately he was let go after the '79 season.

"I just ain't ready for an office yet," Whitey said while waiting on the unemployment line. "I enjoy managing. I enjoy the ballpark. I'm not prepared to give up managing."

It didn't take long for Herzog to find employment. On June 9, 1980, Whitey took over the floundering Cardinals. The team finished fourth that season, but Whitey didn't care. He was sizing up the players, seeing whom he wanted to keep and who he wanted to deal. In the winter of 1980, the shake-up began in St. Louis. Within a five-day span, Herzog dealt 13 players. If he was going to lose, he surmised, he was going to lose with his own players.

"It took a lot of guts for him to do that," said Chuck Hiller, a St. Louis coach.

Whitey Herzog (facing page) is not shy about voicing his opinion, even when he admits a mistake, like trading Keith Hernandez (right).

Earl Weaver (inset left) returned to manage the Orioles in 1985. Dick Howser (inset bottom left) has reason to smile after winning the Series. Inset right: Whitey Herzog and Dick Howser shake hands before the Series. John Tudor (main picture) was another fine acquisition by Herzog.

"He got rid of a lot of popular players and until he proved he would do something, he was going to get the heat. But he never looked back."

He didn't need to. Two years later, Herzog's wholesale trading paid off as the Cards won the division, beat the Braves for the National League pennant and ultimately trimmed the Milwaukee Brewers in the World Series, 4-3, to become World Champions.

"Basically, what Whitey has been able to do is build the kind of team he wants," said Bruce Sutter, the Cardinals' bullpen ace in 1982. "He has always liked to manage teams with speed, as opposed to home-run power. So he came to St. Louis, took a look at the ballpark, and saw that only a few people, like Mike Schmidt, could consistently hit homers here. Whitey put together a team of jackrabbits because that's what he liked."

Despite the huge success of the Cards, Herzog began dismantling them in the 1983 season. On the eve of the trading deadline, he shipped Keith Hernandez to the Mets for Neil Allen and Rick Ownbey. Ken Oberkfell was dispatched to Atlanta for promising pitcher Ken Dayley and utility player Mike Jorgensen. And the off-season of 1984 he dealt George Hendrick for outstanding left-hander John Tudor. But his biggest deal to date saw Jack Clark come East in return for Dave LaPoint, David Green, Jose Uribe and Gary Rajsich. While some of these trades worked out well and others didn't, the only important thing for Herzog is the performance of the team.

"It makes me mad when people ask what this guy's doing or that guy's doing," said Herzog about his trading. "The bottom line is, how is the club doing?"

And one look at the 1985 standings shows St. Louis at the top.

In baseball terms, Kansas City Royals' field boss Dick Howser is called a "players'-manager." Quiet and unassuming, the 49-year-old skipper is a low-key, class act. He is Billy Martin turned inside-out. Never a bad word for anybody, never a criticism. Instead of placing the burden of responsibility on the players, he'll take the burden and place it on himself.

Consider Game Two of the 1985 World Series. The Royals lead 2-1 in the top of the ninth. Bases loaded, two out and starting pitcher Charlie Leibrandt is faltering. With reliever supreme Dan Quisenberry warm, it's a given that "Quiz" will enter the game, lock up the win and knot the Series at one game apiece. But Howser stays with Leibrandt,

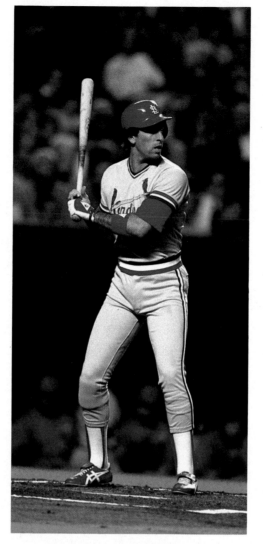

One of Whitey Herzog's greatest deals was acquiring Jack Clark (above) from the San Francisco Giants in the winter of 1984. Clark then ended Tommy Lasorda's (right) season by clouting a game-winning home run in the play-offs.

Terry Pendleton hits a bases-clearing double and the critics are out.

"The easiest thing for me to do would have been to bring in Quisenberry," Howser said. "Then I would have put the bear on his back instead of mine. If Quisenberry came in and they scored that many runs, you don't think everyone would say what a foolish move it was when Leibrandt was pitching so well? You really don't think so?"

Such is the character of Dick Howser. Honesty and diplomacy are two things he's noted for. In retrospect, maybe that's why it's so hard to believe he went to work for George Steinbrenner.

Howser played eight seasons in the major leagues as a utility player before taking the coaching reins of the New York Yankees for 10 seasons. From there, he moved to his alma mater Florida State to become head baseball coach. It was one of the five best college baseball jobs in the country, and Howser was enjoying every minute of it.

"I just coached and recruited," he said. "No teaching and my hardest job was turning away recruits."

He stayed there a year before Steinbrenner coaxed him to take the Yankee job. During a Seminole home game, the dugout phone rang and none other than Steinbrenner was on the other end.

"I guess you read about Billy," George said, regarding Billy Martin's knockout of a marshmallow salesman in the off-season.

"Yeah, I read about him," Howser replied.

"Well, if it's true that he hit the guy," Steinbrenner said, "he's no longer the manager of the Yanks. If it's true, I want you as manager."

In 1980, he guided the Yanks to the East Division championship and a 103-victory season before losing to Kansas City in the League Championship Series. Certainly Howser performed admirably in his first campaign as manager, as only one other first-year field boss in baseball history (Ralph Houk, 109 wins in 1961) won more games. Steinbrenner, however, thanked him for 103 wins by forcing him to "resign", stating privately that the low-key Howser lost control of his club.

"I can be firm if I have to be, I believe in clearing the air," Howser said. "I don't like things hanging because it gets uncontrollable sometimes. I have some rules, but I'm not rule-heavy. I like some discipline, but I don't want to be overly disciplined. If I see a guy out of line, I'll talk to him. I don't believe in threats and I don't like to repeat myself. I like to have a good time, but I take a business-like approach to it because it's (managing) business."

"I'm going into this as a players' manager. I'm not going to be rah-rah, and talking to players doesn't mean I'm always telling them what they want to hear. But I'll answer their questions and talk to them. People say you can't manage that way, but I feel I can."

Maybe George didn't think those attributes were important, but the Kansas City Royals certainly did. On August 31, 1981, he was named Royals' skipper and a happy marriage ensued. What transpired from there were two second place finishes, a division crown, and then, in 1985, the World Championship.

Who says nice guys finish last?

THE PLAYOFFS

As the Mets and Cardinals battled down the stretch to see which team would win the Eastern Division flag and ultimately face the Dodgers in the playoffs, many Los Angeles players privately confided that they would rather play the Cardinals. Power, the Dodgers felt, could bust open a short series and the Mets, with Gary Carter, Darryl Strawberry and company were stocked.

The Cardinals, on the other hand, were a team built on speed, speed and more speed. As former St. Louis pitcher Joaquin Andujar said early in the season, "We have seven leadoff hitters and two power hitters, me and Jack Clark."

As the Dodgers suspected, power decided the playoff series. But to their dismay, the little sticks of the Cards provided most of the dynamite.

The memory of Bobby Thomson's dramatic playoff home run off Ralph Branca in 1951 is the measuring stick by which other post-season dramatics are compared. And as far as the Cardinals are concerned, Thomson's "shot heard 'round the world" paled to the late-inning heroics provided by Ozzie Smith in Game Five and Jack Clark in Game Six.

With the series even at two games, the Dodgers sent Fernando Valenzuela to duel Bob Forsch in Game Five. Consecutive walks to Willie McGee and Smith and a bases-clearing double by Tommy Herr staked the Cards to a 2-0 advantage in the first inning. Los Angeles knotted the game at two in the fourth on a single by Ken Landreaux and two-run homer by Bill Madlock.

Both teams then matched zeros through the eighth, setting the stage for a climactic finish in the ninth. Dodgers reliever Tom Niedenfuer retired McGee to open the final frame, but up stepped Smith, the usually light-hitting shortstop who's paid two million dollars annually to turn double plays and go deep in the hole and throw out a batter. Smith demonstrated to everyone that he is more than just "The Wizard of Oz" because of his fielding. He promptly belted the first offering from Niedenfuer, an inside fastball, over the wall in right field to send the Cardinals to Los Angeles needing just one win to earn a trip to the World Series.

Even more ironic than Smith just hitting the home run was that he did it batting lefthanded. It was the first home run for Smith batting lefthanded in his career.

Previous pages: Darrell Porter (left) batted .267 in the N.L.C.S. for the Cards while Fernando Valenzuela (right) won the opening game of the play-offs for the Dodgers. Terry Pendleton (left) hit only .208, but drove in four runs in the play-offs.

"Players make the manager," said St. Louis skipper Whitey Herzog after the game, "and in Ozzie Smith, I have probably the greatest shortstop who ever played the game."

"I'm a better offensive player than I'm given credit for," Smith said. "I worked hard with weights in the off-season to improve my upper body strength."

Clark doesn't need to improve his upper body strength to send baseballs into orbit. With 22 home runs in the regular season, Clark is a bona fide power hitter. And in the top of the ninth inning, with Los Angeles leading 5-4 and runners on second and third. Clark stepped to the plate. With the righthander Niedenfuer on the mound and slumping Andy Van Slyke on deck, logic said walk Clark. Dodgers manager Tom Lasorda said pitch to Clark.

Once again, Niedenfuer threw the first pitch down Broadway and Clark rocketed the ball into the leftfield stands for the game-winning homer that sent the Cards into the Series and the Dodgers onto the golf course.

"The only way that thing would have stayed in the park was if it hit the Goodyear blimp and dropped straight down," said a downcast Niedenfuer after the game.

"I just wanted to make contact and hit the ball hard and hopefully just tie the score," Clark said. "But as it worked out, I got all of it. This was the greatest home run of my career and of my life."

The beginning of the series lacked the drama of Games Five and Six, yet still proved to be an interesting matchup.

Game One was the antithesis of the game plan everyone expected. Most of the season the Dodgers were the big play club, relying on strong pitching and waiting for the long ball to decide the outcome. The Cardinals, meanwhile, scratched and clawed for their runs, bunting, stealing bases and capitalizing on errors to make up for their lack of power.

The aces of each staff, Fernando Valenzuela and John Tudor hooked up to keep things scoreless through three innings. In the fourth, the Dodgers drew first blood when Cards third baseman Terry Pendleton couldn't handle Bill Madlock's grounder. Madlock then shocked the Cards by stealing second and scoring on a bloop single by Pedro Guerrero. A typical Cardinal run.

Los Angeles chased Tudor in the sixth on a double by Madlock, an intentional walk to Guerrero and a run-scoring single by Mike Scioscia. Candy Maldonado pulled another Cardinals trick by successfully executing the squeeze play as the Dodgers triumphed in Game One 4-1.

Before Game Two, the loquacious Joaquin Andujar went out of his way to praise his mound opponent Orel Hershiser.

"Hershiser's one of the best right-handed pitchers in baseball. All you guys

Cesar Cedeno (below) was a late-season pickup by the Cards, and here, in Game Five, he connects against Valenzuela. Nothing went right for the Blue Jays after taking a 3-1 series lead.

This was to be a record-breaking series before it even began, as the league championship was extended from five to seven games. But after just two innings of Game Four, records fell like rocks in a landslide.

The Cards erupted for nine second-inning runs en route to a 12-2 romp of the Dodgers to square the series at two games each. Records shattered in the second-frame debacle included most runs (9), most hits (8), most official at-bats (12) and Jerry Reuss' seven runs allowed. Every Cardinal in the starting lineup either scored or got a base hit.

But perhaps the wildest and most talked about occurence happened before the contest, when the automatic tarpaulin rolled onto the legs of Vince Coleman during warmups. With Coleman writhing in pain and with thousands of pounds of pressure on the outfielder's legs, the machine was finally stopped and reversed. Coleman, however, was carried off on a stretcher and missed the rest of the playoffs.

Luckily the Cardinals were victorious without him. The same could not be said about the World Series.

(media) go with (Dwight) Gooden. I go with Hershiser. He's smart, got a good slider and a good sinker. He's young and a good hitter too."

How prophetic. Not only did Hershiser go the distance in an 8-2 Los Angeles romp, but the 27-year-old drove in a run. Ken Landreaux paced the Dodgers' attack with three hits while Greg Brock smacked a two-run homer.

Andujar's pitching line? Four and a third innings pitched, eight hits, six runs.

Game Three. Back on the carpet at Busch Stadium and when the Cards are on the artificial turf, they're a different team. The change of scenery was immediately apparent as St. Louis scored a pair of runs off Bob Welch in both the first and second innings to jump to a 4-0 advantage. The speed of Vince Coleman came into play for the first time in the series as both Los Angeles errors were a result of failed pick-off plays.

The top three of the Cards' lineup, Coleman, Willie McGee and Tommy Herr, stifled in Los Angeles, cracked two hits apiece. Danny Cox held the Dodgers to two runs and recorded the victory with relief help from Ken Dayley.

It was an improbable finish by an improbable team. The Kansas City Royals were not supposed to win their division, especially after trailing California late in the season. They weren't supposed to triumph in the playoffs, especially when the Blue Jays took a commanding lead in the league championship series.

They were the second weakest offensive team in the league, a club made up of George Brett and a bunch of no-names (excluding, of course, Buddy Biancalana, whose name was chronicled by David Letterman because of his futility at the bat), a team held together by a solid pitching staff and the experience of victories past.

But these Royals were also a special team. Led by one chief (George Brett) and a reservation full of Indians, the Royals did something only four teams ever did in a seven-game series. They rallied from a 3-1 deficit in games and scalped the Jays. And they did it in Toronto.

"When we were down 3-1, it was hard to imagine coming back and winning," said Royals second baseman Frank White. "I mean, Toronto is so good. When we won the pennant in 1980, I thought there would be plenty more. Then, when no more came, I thought my time had gone. I got frustrated early in this series because it always seemed the last few years that we lacked the one hitter or the one pitcher we needed. Now, to see this, well, it's hard to express what it

Frank White's face shows the strain as he takes a mighty swing (main picture). George Brett (inset), the star of the A.L.C.S., races home from third base.

means. No one expected us to do it. I guess that makes it even sweeter."

"It had nothing to do with pressure, nothing to do with choking," said Toronto's third baseman Rance Mulliniks. "They executed when they had to, and their pitching was phenomenal, especially in the last four games. And we just didn't get the hits when we had to. We had our chances, but we left too many men on."

The same could not be said after Game One, when Toronto's Dave Stieb showed why he has started the last two All-Star games. The Blue Jays' right-hander coasted to an easy 6-1 win, yielding only three hits through eight innings. Tony Fernandez and Ernie Whitt each drove on a pair of runs to stake the Jays to a 1-0 series advantage.

As easy as the Blue Jays won the first encounter, that's how tough it was for the Royals to lose Game Two.

Kansas City jumped to a 3-0 lead in the third inning when Willie Wilson added a two-run homer to a first inning run. But the Blue Jays stormed back with single runs in the third and eighth sandwiched around a two-run fifth frame to take a 4-3 advantage into the ninth.

The Royals evened the contest in the top of the ninth and took the lead on Frank White's single in the tenth off reliever Tom Henke. The game seemed in the bag, what with the number one stopper in baseball over the past five years, Dan Quisenberry, on the mound. But a streak of inglorious play, including an infield hit that should have been scored an error, and a misplay on a pickoff attempt, paved the way for Al Oliver's game-winning single. The victory not only gave the Blue Jays a commanding 2-0 series advantage, but extended Kansas City's post-season losing streak to 10 games.

"I think it's incredible," said Quisenberry about the Royals' dubious skein. "You'd think that in one game we'd win 7-1, that we'd have 15 hits, a lot of wall balls, and shut them down. But we don't do that. We play two out of three close, but we don't win."

"If a home run beats you, or two line drives and a home run, that's different," explained Royals manager Dick Howser about the way his club lost Game Two. "But to get beat like that..."

Luckily for the Royals, George Brett plays on their team. The Kansas City third baseman, who concluded possibly his best major league campaign, nearly singlehandedly cut the K.C. deficit in half. The nine-time all-star went 4-for-4, clouted two home runs and scored four runs as Steve Farr pitched four-and-a-third innings of perfect relief in a 6-5 Royals win.

Kansas City suffered another gut-wrenching defeat in Game Four to put the Blue Jays one game away from a World Series berth. Charlie Leibrandt cruised along for eight innings, clinging to a one-run lead, when disaster struck in the ninth. The Royals' veteran southpaw ran out of steam in the final frame, yielding a walk and a tying double before Quisenberry took over. Instead of extinguishing the rally, the ace reliever proved to be a gas can. Al Oliver enjoyed an encore performance as the seasoned campaigner ripped a two-bagger to give the Jays a 3-1 victory and a seemingly insurmountable 3-1 series lead.

The Royals salvaged at least a trip back to Toronto to continue the series when Danny Jackson scattered eight hits in whitewashing the Jays 2-0. George Brett knocked in the game-winning run with his 18th career RBI in the first inning, tying the all-time mark held by Reggie Jackson.

The series moved to Toronto for the final two games, but the momentum seemed to remain with the Royals. And once again it was Brett who proved to be the catalyst for Kansas City.

Brett hit his third home run of the series and his third off Toronto's Doyle Alexander to break a 2-2 deadlock in the fifth frame of Game Six. While Brett may have been the catalyst, Kansas City reserved the spotlight for the most unlikely hero. Buddy Biancalana, laughed at nationally by David Letterman for his "hitting exploits," went 2-for-4 with an RBI double in the sixth to give the Royals an insurance run.

"It's been real frustrating," Biancalana admitted about his poor hitting. "I got up in the morning and said, 'Here's my chance. Don't let it pass you by. There aren't many opportunities like this.'"

The Royals were thrilled just to have the opportunity to play a seventh game, and their enthusiasm transformed itself into runs on the field of play. Kansas City quickly jumped on Jays starter Dave Stieb for single runs in the second and fourth before blowing the game open with a four-run outburst in the sixth. Jim Sundberg, playing in his first post-season series, added a base-clearing triple to his second inning RBI single to give the Royals a 6-1 lead. The Blue Jays did add a meaningless ninth inning run off Charlie Leibrandt, but their fate was sealed.

Nobody thought the Royals could bounce back from a 3-1 deficit. But then again, 1985 was an improbable season for the Royals.

The Blue Jays didn't get many breaks in their series with K.C., including this disputed call.

Cards catcher Tom Nieto shows the ball to the umpire, but it's too late as Jim Sundberg slides home safely.

THE WORLD SERIES

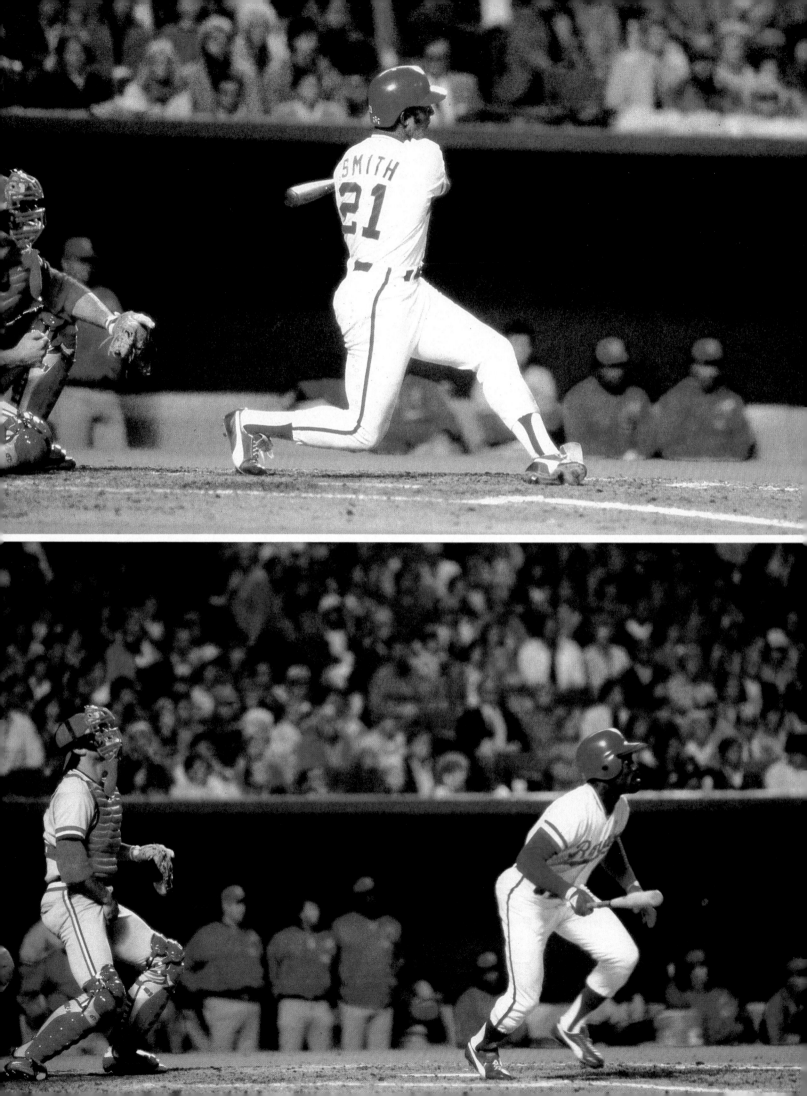

This was called the Interstate 70 Series, but heading into the 1985 Fall Classic, the St. Louis Cardinals and the Kansas City Royals had more similarities than just residing under the Missouri state banner. In fact, the World Series was aptly named because it had a series of twisting subplots and interesting story lines.

Consider the most obvious items. Both teams are from Missouri, making the Classic the first All-Missouri Series since 1944. Both teams also overcame the odds in the league championship series as the Cardinals and Royals rebounded from two game deficits to prevail.

But the Cards and Royals were intertwined more deeply than just the aforementioned. Consider Whitey Herzog, the St. Louis skipper. The White Rat used to be employed by the Royals, and despite accumulating a 410-304 record and winning three division titles while at the helm, Kansas City fired Herzog following the 1979 season.

Consider Kansas City outfielder Lonnie Smith, who became a star under the guidance of Herzog. Smith started the year in a Cardinals uniform and was traded to the Royals for a minor-leaguer in May.

Consider the Royals' pinch-hitter Dane Iorg. A utility infielder for the Cardinals in the late '70s, Iorg starred in the 1982 World Series in which the Cardinals won. He too was dealt to the Royals, this time in May of '84.

Consider the Cardinals' starting catcher, Darrell Porter. The former league championship series MVP played for the Royals in the late '70s before signing with St. Louis as a free agent.

Consider the Cardinals' pinch-hitter Steve Braun. Braun also had a stint in a Royals uniform and still lives in Kansas City in the off-season.

So before the first pitch of the I-70 Series, the Show-Me-State Series or whatever else you want to call it, the 1985 version of the World Series contained more sub-plots than *General Hospital*.

Still, the Cards were stacked against the Royals. Kansas City, we were told, had no chance to win the Series. St. Louis was rested, their ace pitcher and baseball's hottest hurler the final three months of the season, John Tudor, was set for three starts. The Royals' best pitcher, 21-year-old Bret Saberhagen, was doubtful after an injury in the league championship series. Following George Brett, the Royals lineup looked like it was made up of a bunch of little league hitters.

Darryl Motley (bottom left) and Lonnie Smith (top left) took mighty swings against John Tudor (right).

And despite all the odds and all the predictions of doom, the Royals capped their season in a breathtaking, come-from-behind fashion, as they rebounded from a 3-1 deficit to take home the silverware. Maybe that's why saying the Kansas City Royals are baseball's 1985 World Champions sounds strange.

And the way they won it is even stranger. It's the seventh game of a series tied at three. It was supposed to be the quintessential pitching matchup. John Tudor vs. Bret Saberhagen. The guileful, crafty, cerebral Tudor against the power

and poise of Saberhagen. But what it turned out to be was more reminiscent of a Stanley Cup hockey game than a World Series contest. Before it was over, Tudor was bombed, Herzog was thumbed, and Joaquin Andujar was bummed. The final score: 11-0, Royals.

History will remember not only the final score, but how it got that way. Saberhagen pitched another sterling post-season game, becoming the youngest player to receive the World Series MVP. Tudor, who won 20-of-21 regular season games and three-of-four

post-season starts, was rocked for five runs in only two-and-one-third innings. Herzog, meanwhile, was tossed in the six-run Royals fifth frame and Andujar was ejected, then restrained, after attacking umpire Don Denkinger following a ball-strike dispute.

"In a 10-0 game in the seventh game of the World Series, there are no close calls," said Cardinals outfielder Andy Van Slyke about Andujar's theatrics. "I felt sorry for the kids around the country more than anything else. There were 10-12 million kids around the country who was forced to play without the injured Vince Coleman, the Cardinals' offensive catalyst. "Thirteen runs in seven games. That's almost a disgrace. But they had enough pitching to win the series."

They didn't begin that way, though. In Game One, Tudor dueled Danny Jackson and the night started in K.C.'s favor. In the second inning, Jim Sundberg walked and scored on singles by Darryl Motley and Steve Balboni. St. Louis came right back in the third on a free pass to Terry Pendleton, a single by Porter, a sacrifice fly by Tudor and a groundout by Willie McGee.

In the fourth frame, the Cards took the lead for good on back-to-back doubles by Tito Landrum and Cesar

Tommy Herr (above) steps on the bag to start a double play. Bret Saberhagen (right) was the Series M.V.P.

watching, and now they think that's the way a major leaguer acts."

That's not why the Cardinals became the fifth team in major league history to lose a series after leading three games to one. Hitting, or lack thereof, proved to be their undoing.

"We just couldn't hit worth a damn," said St. Louis manager Whitey Herzog,

Former St. Louis pitcher Joaquin Andujar touched off an embarrassing situation in Game Seven as he charged home plate umpire Don Denkinger following a disputed call. Andujar (far right) is restrained by teammates from going after Denkinger.

Cedeno. The Red Birds added an insurance run in the ninth off Dan Quisenberry and Game One was the Cards', 3-1.

Game Two was perfect night for second-guessers and people with 20-20 hindsight. As in the opening game, Kansas City tallied first, scoring a pair of runs in the fourth inning off Cards starter Danny Cox.

Meanwhile, Royals lefthander Charlie Leibrandt was cruising along, allowing but two hits the first eight innings. In the Cardinals' final at-bat, Willie McGee broke a string of 13 hitters retired in a row by belting a double. Ozzie Smith and Tommy Herr followed with a groundout and a fly out respectively, to bring the Royals within one out of

knotting the series. Then Jack Clark grounded a single in the hole to score McGee and went to third on Landrum's double. Leibrandt intentionally walked Cedeno to load the bases.

In the bullpen, warm and ready to enter the game, was Quisenberry, arguably the major league's top relief pitcher. It was a situation that cried for the A.L.'s Fireman of the Year winner four of the last five seasons. But instead, Royals manager Dick Howser stayed with a tiring Leibrandt and Pendleton stroked a base-clearing double to give the Cards a 4-2 victory and a commanding 2-0 edge in games.

"It was Leibrandt's game to win or lose," said Howser. "He wasn't losing his stuff, his control was good, his stuff was

great. He was in complete command."

"I just went to the plate looking for a good pitch and trying to hit the ball somewhere," Pendleton said. "His (Leibrandt's) pitches didn't have the pop that they had in the earlier innings."

"You can't play a better game than we played," said Kansas City's George Brett. "We played fantastic. We played good enough to win both nights and we lost both. But this is the toughest way to lose a ball game. I'd rather lose 6-1, and say we got our butts kicked and say we'll come back and get them the next time. But these are killers."

With the Royals down two games and traveling to hostile Busch Stadium for Game Three, Kansas City pinned its hopes on a 21-year-old kid who'd been knocked around in the league championship series. Bret Saberhagen was hit on the foot and hand in separate games against the Toronto Blue Jays and didn't make it past the fifth inning in either start. Before the game, Saberhagen, who became the youngest pitcher to start a World Series contest since Jim Palmer hurled in the 1966 Series, showed no concern about pressure or his youthfulness. "The last game is over and done," he said. "There's nothing we can do about it. And I may be 21, but it seems like my body is 25."

Saberhagen's birth certificate reads 21, he says he feels 25, but watching him pitch makes him look like he's a 30-year-old veteran. Even the Cardinals would agree, especially after the youngster pitched a six-hit complete game in the Royals' 6-1 win to cut the Cards' lead in half, 2-1.

While Saberhagen was throwing goose eggs, the Royals finally began hitting, scoring a pair of runs in the fourth and fifth frame off Joaquin Andujar. Frank

Frank White (facing page) tries to keep Willie McGee from straying too far off second base. Jack Clark (above) shows his home run swing. Danny Cox compiled a 1.29 e.r.a. for the Series.

White, who was switched to the clean-up slot by Dick Howser prior to the game, did most of the damage as he clouted a two-run shot in the fifth and added an RBI double in the seventh.

"Baseball is a game of dreams, and people dream about something like this," White said after the game. "But I never dared to dream that I would be batting fourth in a World Series or that I'd hit a homer in the Series."

Game Four looked like the beginning of the end for the Royals. With John Tudor on the mound and painting the corners of the plate like Michelangelo, the Cards easily took a commanding 3-1 lead in games. Tudor merely allowed five hits, walking one as St. Louis whitewashed Kansas City 3-0.

"Tudor is much more of a pitcher than when he was in the American League," said losing manager Dick Howser. "He changes speeds well, and he still has a good fastball. He isn't going to 'walk his way' out of a game, and they aren't going to kick it around behind him. So you need four or five hits in a row to do something against him."

"I did just about everything right," Tudor said after the contest. "I threw the

ball in, out, up and down and had a good changeup. Tonight, I threw as well as I'm capable of throwing."

All Tudor needed was a single run and Tito Landrum supplied that with an opposite field homer off loser Bud Black. Willie McGee added another home run. The Cards tacked on an insurance run in the fifth on a typical St. Louis play. With one out, Pendleton tripled to center, bringing Tom Nieto to the plate. On a full-count, Whitey Herzog had the suicide squeeze play on and Nieto bunted the ball perfectly as Pendleton scooted home.

"I thought the 3-and-2 bunt was a pretty high percentage play," said Herzog. "Even if they pitch out and get Pendleton at the plate, Nieto gets a walk

out of it, and we get our pitcher to the plate next, which means, at worst, that we still have a 2-0 lead and we get to start the next inning with the top of our batting order."

In Game Five, Whitey Herzog had no problems with strategy. Before the game was too innings old, the Royals, hanging on for their Series lives, broke out to a 4-1 advantage. And with Danny Jackson pitching perhaps his finest game of the season, Kansas City prevailed 6-1 to cut the Cards Series lead to three games to two.

"We came into this game happy. We didn't think about being eliminated," said

The Royals added insurance runs in the eighth and ninth to put the game away, but not before Cards rookie reliever Todd Worrell made World Series history by fanning all six Royals batters he faced in a two-inning stint.

Game Six was baseball at its nailbiting best. For seven innings, Charlie Leibrandt and Danny Cox matched zeros as the suspense grew. Both teams figured that the first team to score would win this one. And in the bottom of the seventh, it appeared the Royals would send this series to a seventh and final game. Steve Balboni walked and Buddy Biancalana followed with a two-out single. With Dan

George Brett (left) paced the Royals' regulars, hitting .370. Tito Landrum (above) watches his home run in Game Four. Charlie Leibrandt (right) lost a heartbreaker in Game Two. Brian Harper's pinch-hit (overleaf) gave St. Louis a 1-0 lead in Game Six.

Royals centerfielder Willie Wilson. "Hey, we came back after we were two games down in the American League Championship Series and we're going to come back from two games down in this one. The reason? It's simple. We want our World Series rings."

Wilson played a part in working toward his goal by teaming with Lonnie Smith for first inning singles to produce a run. The Cardinals tied the game in the bottom of the first on back-to-back doubles by Tommy Herr and Jack Clark.

Wilson helped the Royals put the game away in the second when he cracked a two-run triple off loser Bob Forsch as K.C. jumped to a 4-1 advantage.

"Forsch just couldn't get his breaking ball over the plate," said Herzog. "Wilson got fastballs to hit in the first two innings and Willie can hit a fastball."

Quisenberry warm in the pen and Leibrandt due up, everybody expected a pinch-hitter. Everybody, that is, except Dick Howser.

"If we'd had a guy on third with less than two out, I'd have hit for Leibrandt," said the Royals' skipper. "But I wasn't going to take a guy who was pitching a two-hit shutout for anything other than that kind of situation."

So Leibrandt stepped up the plate, and three swings later, stood on the mound ready for the Cardinals' eighth. And for Leibrandt and the Royals, it was a disappointing eighth.

Quickly, the Cardinals had Terry Pendleton on second and Cesar Cedeno on first with two outs. Herzog immediately sent righty hitter Brian Harper to bat for Darrell Porter and on a 1-2 count, the pinch-hitter blooped a broken-bat

single to centerfield to give St. Louis a 1-0 lead. In two more innings, the Cardinals would be World Champs. Or would they?

In the bottom of the ninth, Jorge Orta bounced a high-hopper to the right side, where Jack Clark fielded it and tossed to reliever Todd Worrell for an easy out. But before you could say, "One out and two to go," first-base umpire Don Denkinger called Orta safe and the rally was on.

Balboni followed with a single and the Royals threatened. Worrell, on in relief, then pounced on a Jim Sundberg bunt and forced Orta at third. With pinch-hitter Hal McRae at the plate, though, Porter mishandled a Worrell pitch moving both runners into scoring

position. The Cards walked McRae intentionally to load the bases.

Then the irony started. Howser sent Dane Iorg to pinch-hit knowing full well that Iorg batted over .500 in a Cardinals' uniform in the 1982 World Series. And on a 1-1 count, Iorg delivered a base hit to rightfield. Like a springed coil, Andy Van Slyke raced in and slingshotted the ball toward home plate, trying to stop the winning run from scoring. But the throw was late and the Royals were able to snare victory from the mouth of defeat, sending the World Series to Game Seven.

"All I knew was that I was in a situation that you dream about as a child," said Iorg. "To be hitting in the ninth inning of a World Series game with the bases loaded and victory on the line.

To get a chance to fulfill that dream, regardless of what happened, was special to me."

Tommy Herr (facing page) hit only .154 in the Series, while John Tudor (top center) lost the finale. Frank White (above) and Willie Wilson (left) contributed to the Royals victory.

But not to the Cardinals. After all, they got embarrassed in the seventh game of the World Series, not only on the scoreboard (11-0), but with their sportsmanship. Even now, it still sounds weird. The Kansas City Royals, 1985 World Champions.

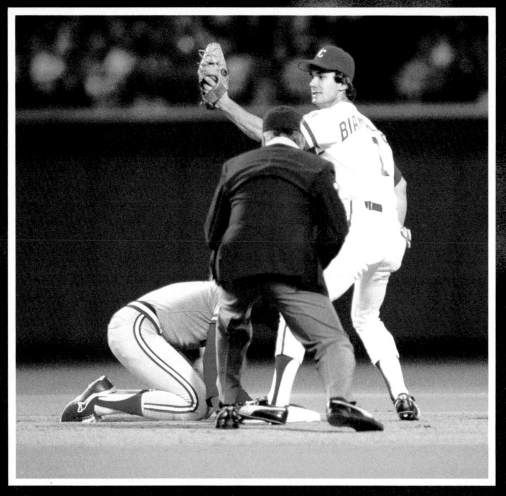

Buddy Biancalana slaps
the tag on (left) while Bret
Saberhagen (bottom left)
acknowledges the fans in
K.C. Main picture: Darryl
Motley slides into second
as Ozzie Smith fires the
ball to complete a double
play.

THE TEAMS

Gary Carter (inset) chases a pop while Ozzie Virgil pops Andre Dawson (right) at home plate.

New York Mets

Perhaps no team in baseball feels as snakebit as the New York Mets. For the past two seasons, no National League team has won as many games. Unfortunately, the Cubs of '84 and the Cards of '85 have put together better individual seasons. But not too many clubs would feel snakebit if they employed Dwight Gooden.

Not since Bob Gibson toyed with batters in 1968, has any pitcher so thoroughly dominated the league as Dwight Gooden. Posting a 24-4 record, the Doctor led the majors with a microscopic 1.53 e.r.a. while striking out 268 and netting 16 complete games. He

youngest starting staff in baseball. Twenty-four-year-old Ron Darling joined Gooden in the All-Star game (16-6, 2.90 e.r.a.) while 22-year-old Sid Fernandez (best ratio of hits to innings pitched and strikeouts to innings pitched in baseball) and 22-year-old Rick Aguilera (10-7) joined the club early in the season to form a solid foursome.

Entering the 1985 season, the Mets were billed as a powerful hitting team and, after a slow start, they didn't let anyone down. Gary Carter hit a career high 32 homers to go with 100 RBI while Keith Hernandez batted over .300 for the fifth time in his career.

Injuries, however, probably cost the Mets a chance at the pennant.

due to shoulder problems.

Still, the Mets won 98 games, the third highest in baseball and still didn't make post-season play. Maybe that's why they feel snakebit.

STADIUM: Shea Stadium. With airplanes flying overhead from La Guardia Airport, Shea Stadium is known to be a pitcher's ballpark. Due to poor hitting background, power pitchers have flourished.

DIMENSIONS: 338 feet down the lines, 410 to centerfield. Outfield fence measures 8 feet.

TURF: Natural grass.

CAPACITY: 55,300

topped off his sensational season by unanimously winning the Cy Young award and, at 20, became the youngest recipient of the prestigious trophy.

Gooden was not the only budding star in a rotation that boasted the

Darryl Strawberry missed seven weeks and still hit 29 home runs. Mookie Wilson, the catalyst on offense, sat out two months with shoulder surgery and Bruce Berenyi, counted on to be the third starter, pitched three games all season

Roger McDowell (above) emerged as an important addition to the Mets staff as he became the righthanded relief ace. Jesse Orosco (facing page) struggled with a sore arm in 1985.

Hubie Brooks (inset left) went to Montreal in the Gary Carter trade and drove in 100 runs. Darryl Strawberry (main picture) hit 29 HRs despite missing seven weeks. Dwight Gooden (insets top and bottom right) overpowered National League hitters.

Montreal Expos

When Gary Carter was traded by the Expos in the winter of '84, Montreal fans mourned the loss of their hero. Then they took it out on Expos management by not showing up at the ballpark. Montreal attendance was down considerably and they averaged 4,000 fewer fans than the year by recording an 18-5 record while Joe Hesketh was in the race for rookie honors until a broken leg ended his season. The bullpen, however, was the key. Jeff Reardon led the majors in saves with 41 and earned the nickname "The Terminator." Tim Burke merely emerged as a star, complementing Reardon with nine wins and eight saves.

St. Louis Cardinals

If anyone other than manager Whitey Herzog had suggested the Cardinals could win more games than any team in baseball in 1985, that person might have been placed on the mentally disabled list. And despite "expert" predictions of a last-place finish, St. Louis won 101 games,

league average. However, if you asked Montreal management to make the Carter trade again, they probably would.

Despite the loss of Carter, the Expos surprised many by finishing a strong third in the East. Hubie Brooks, one of four newcomers for Carter, compiled the best offensive statistics for a National League shortstop since Ernie Banks by knocking in 100 runs. The other major contributor of The Trade was pitcher Floyd Youmans, a former teammate of Dwight Gooden in high school.

Youmans arrived in Montreal at mid-season and displayed the stuff of a winner; a 90 mile-per-hour fastball and a sharp breaking deuce.

Pitching proved a bright spot for the Expos all season. Bryn Smith had a career

Hitting was another story. Montreal finished fifth from the bottom in average and tenth in RBI although Tim Raines placed third in batting with a .320 average.

What the Expos needed for a division title was a Gary Carter – or at least another Hubie Brooks.

STADIUM: Olympic Stadium. The stadium was originally erected for the 1976 Summer Olympic Games.

DIMENSIONS: 325 feet down the lines, 375 feet in the power alleys and 408 feet to centerfield. The outfield fence measures 12 feet.

TURF: Artificial surface.

CAPACITY: 59,149.

Andre Dawson (above left) was troubled with sore knees. Willie McGee (above) led the N.L. with 216 hits. Bryn Smith (facing page) emerged as a star pitcher in '85.

the most in baseball and the most by a Cardinals team since its 1967 championship season.

What propelled the Cards to the top was a high-flying running game that produced 314 stolen bases, fourth highest total in major league history. Not only were the numbers staggering, but opposing pitchers were staggered as St. Louis led the National League with a .264 batting average.

Nobody provided the Cardinals with more of a jump start than rookie

Tim Raines slides safely under the tag of Wally Backman (main picture). Ozzie Smith (inset top) and manager Whitey Herzog (inset above) had a lot to be happy about.

swept the pitching awards if it weren't for a kid named Gooden. After a dismal 1-7 start, Tudor won 20 of his next 21 decisions and finished the season with a sparkling 1.93 e.r.a., 10 shutouts and 14 complete games. Joaquin Andujar, since traded to Oakland, joined Tudor as a 20-game winner despite an abysmal finish,

Willie McGee (left) responded with an M.V.P year in 1985, while Tommy Herr (above and facing page) produced his best offense season, batting .302 with 110 RBI.

and Danny Cox chipped in an unexpected 18 victories to give St. Louis the most wins among its top three starters in baseball.

Only Whitey Herzog could have thought it.

STADIUM: Busch Stadium. The Cardinals' home, opened May 12, 1966, can easily be distinguished by the twin arches outside the left field fence and the enormous power alleys that encompass the outfield. Due to the dimensions and the artificial turf field, St. Louis is almost forced into finding speedy, rangy outfielders to cut off baseballs hit into the alleys.

DIMENSIONS: 338 feet down the lines and 401 feet to centerfield. The outfield fence measures 8 feet.

TURF: Artificial.

CAPACITY: 60,000.

sensation Vince Coleman. Sent to the minors in spring training, Coleman resurfaced in May and set an all-time rookie stolen base record with 110. Coleman wasn't alone, though. Willie McGee (56 steals), Andy Van Slyke (34), Tommy Herr (31) and Ozzie Smith (31) kept pitchers more occupied with first base than with home plate. The stolen bases provided a springboard for tremendous offensive seasons by Herr (110 RBI), McGee (.353 average, 82 RBI) and Jack Clark (22 HR, 87 RBI).

While St. Louis baserunners ran rings around the opposition, Cardinal hurlers were the second best unit in the National League with a team earned run average of 3.10. No unit was more surprising than the bullpen, which lost stalwart Bruce Sutter and his 45 saves to free agency. Herzog, however, concocted the "Bullpen by Committee" and among Jeff Lahti, Ken Dayley, Todd Worrell, Bill Campbell and Ricky Horton accumulated 40 saves and amazingly did not lose a lead in the ninth inning.

One pitcher that didn't need much relief was John Tudor, who would have

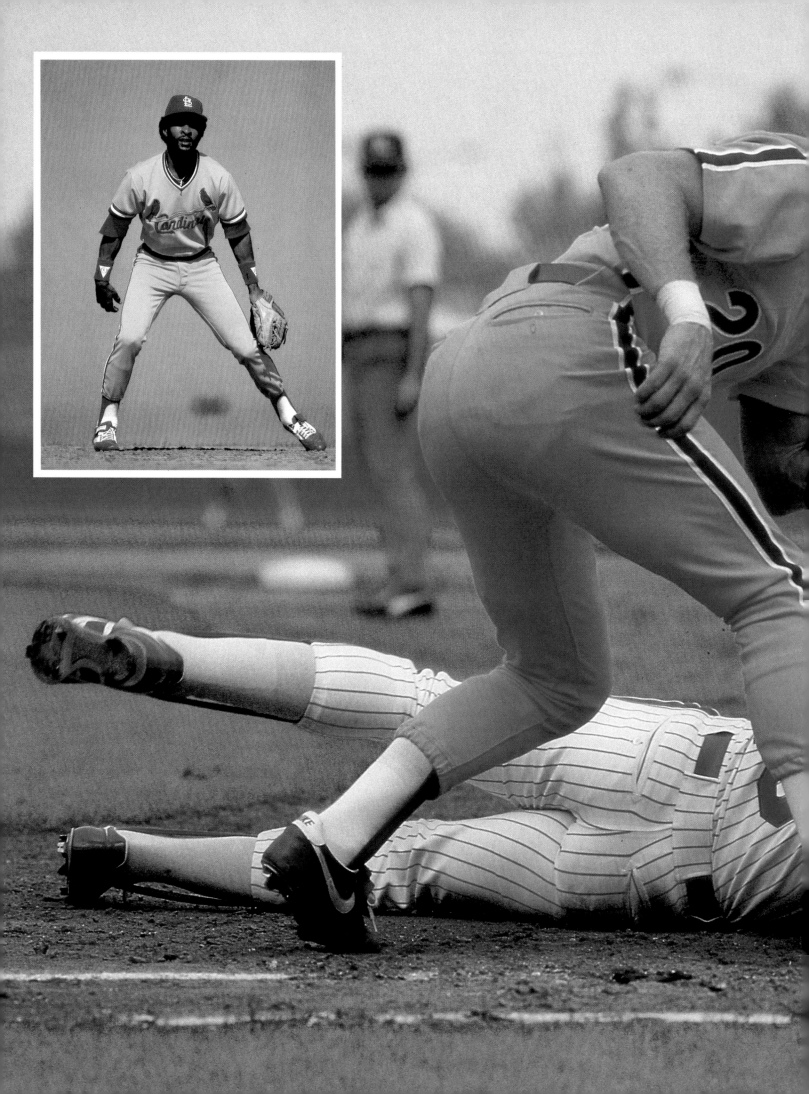

Mike Schmidt, at first base for the Phillies, puts a tag on George Foster (main picture), and (inset top) slides to second base as Santana delivers the ball to first for a double play. Inset above: Cardinals' John Tudor; (inset top left) Ozzie Smith.

Philadelphia Phillies

When the '85 season began, the Phillies were expected to be the kind of ballclub the St. Louis turned out to be – a speedy, record-breaking team. The top three men in the lineup, Jeff Stone, Juan Samuel and Von Hayes, were being counted on to steal close to 200 bases and create havoc on the basepaths. Although Samuel posted outstanding numbers and even fielded well, Stone found himself exiled to the minors after a horrible start and Hayes never approached his '84 output.

But it was not only the speed game that doomed the Phillies to fifth place and their worst finish since 1973.

Juan Samuel (left) posted outstanding numbers offensively and even surprised the Phillies by improving his defense. Steve Carlton (above) spent time on the disabled list for the first time in his career.

The graybeards of the pitching staff, Steve Carlton and Jerry Koosman, the oldest pitchers in the National League, pitched as if they wanted to make room on the roster for youngsters. Carlton, 41, found a home on the disabled list for much of the season (the first time in his career he was disabled) and compiled a dismal 1-8 record. Koosman, Carlton's senior by two years, also spent time on the shelf and his 4.62 e.r.a. may have injured his ego, among other things. And

38-year-old Kent Tekulve, an early season pickup, failed to be a stopper in the pen as his 10 losses indicate.

Many felt Mike Schmidt's career was history as the perennial home run champ battled to keep his average above his weight the first half of the season. After a shift to first base, though, Schmidt rebounded to hit 33 round-trippers and record the highest average (.277) of any Phils starting player.

While Schmidt struggled early, Glenn Wilson produced some big numbers and represented the Phils in the all-star game. Wilson almost justified the Phillies' trading relief ace Willie Hernandez for him just prior to the '84 season with his 100 plus RBI.

STADIUM: Veterans Stadium. The Phillies' home has long been noted as a hitter's paradise with the long ball an essential component.

DIMENSIONS: 330 feet down the lines, 408 feet to centerfield. The outfield fence measures 12 feet.

TURF: Artificial surface.

CAPACITY: 66,744.

Pittsburgh Pirates

If ever a baseball city suffered through an off-year, it was Pittsburgh in 1985. Not only did the Pirates compile the most futile record in the major leagues, the worst attendance mark, and the highest turnover in talent, but the city of Pittsburgh became the center of the baseball drug controversy which cast a pall over the sport. To put it mildly, it was not a good year for Pittsburgh baseball.

As it became apparent that the Pirates were destined for a spot in the cellar, the Pittsburgh brass began a garage sale on all its high-priced veteran players. Gone from the beginning of the season were Bill Madlock (Los Angeles), John Candelaria, George Hendrick and Al Holland (California).

Imported were a slew of young, untested talent like Mike Brown, Sid Bream, R.J. Reynolds, and Pat Clements. While the results didn't change in the standings, the Pittsburgh franchise got a fresh look for the future along with a new owner, new general manager and new skipper after the season.

The fans go batty at Yankee Stadium (top) while Ron Cey's bat (left) disappointed the Cubs. Tony Pena (facing page) suffered through his worst offensive season as the Pirates finished dead last.

One of the veterans that did remain emerged to win the Comeback Player of the Year. Rick Reuschel, at 37, seemed at the end of his pitching career when the Pirates offered him a one-year contract for 1985. All he did was win 14 games and register a stingy 2.27 e.r.a. Others who contributed productive seasons were second baseman Johnny Ray (.274, 7 HRs, 70 RBI) and rookie centerfielder Joe Orsulak, who finished at .300.

But no one would argue that Pittsburgh, on and off the field, suffered a horrendous season in 1985.

STADIUM: Three Rivers Stadium. The Pirates' home is one of the new, symmetrical parks, equipped with artificial turf.

DIMENSIONS: 335 feet down the lines, 400 feet to centerfield.

TURF: Artificial.

CAPACITY: 58,429.

Chicago Cubs

Two words can easily sum up the Chicago Cubs of 1985 – frustration and disappointment. Disappointment in that the Cubs were virtually a unanimous choice to win the East entering the season and finished 23 1-2 games behind the Cardinals. Frustrating in that a plethora of injuries caused the disappointment.

And no area on the Cubs was decimated more by injuries than the pitching staff. Over the course of the season, the Cubs used 20 pitchers, more than any team in baseball, including a league-high nine rookies.

It gets worse. At one point, Chicago's entire starting rotation – Rick Sutcliffe, Dennis Eckersley, Scott Sanderson, Steve Trout and Dick Ruthven – kept residence on the disabled list. No Chicago pitcher finished with an e.r.a. of under 3.00 and Sutcliffe, the Cy Young winner the previous season, managed only eight victories. Those are some of the reasons the Cubs landed in the second division. The others are on offense.

Thirty-nine-year-old Ron Cey saw his production fall considerably and by season's end, observers were wondering if age hadn't caught up with him in a hurry. Gary Matthews managed only 40 RBI between stints on the disabled list and Bob Dernier, the spark plug of the '84 division winners, ran out of gas in '85.

Not everyone was working on an empty tank, though. Ryne Sandberg, following his MVP season of '84, compiled an even more impressive

Ryne Sandberg (above and facing page) was one of the few players who didn't disappoint the Cubs.

statistical year. Keith Moreland easily had his finest season, batting over .300 and knocking in 106 runs, while Davey Lopes refused to apply to social security by stealing 47 bases one year short of age 40.

Still, disappointment and frustration were the key words in the Windy City.

STADIUM: Wrigley Field. Chicago's stadium is unique in baseball as it's the only one without artificial lighting. The outfield walls are covered with ivy and when the wind blows out, expect a bunch of runs.

DIMENSIONS: 355 feet to leftfield, 400 feet to center, 353 feet to rightfield.

TURF: Natural grass.

CAPACITY: 37,272.

Dave Concepcion jumps away from a sliding Darryl Strawberry (inset top left). Pete Rose (inset far left and main picture) led the Reds to a surprising second place finish. Dave Parker's (inset left) effort was unquestioned in 1985.

Cincinnati Reds

If it wasn't for Pete Rose, the Reds might have been recognized as one of the better teams in baseball. But then again, if it wasn't for Pete Rose, the Reds might *not* have been one of the better teams in baseball.

Sure Rose received much of the attention in his effort to break Ty Cobb's hit record. And sure Rose finally did eclipse the record on an emotional night in September. Equally sure, Rose managed this rag-tag outfit to a second-place finish in the West, their best ending to a season since the days of the Big Red Machine of the mid '70s.

And Rose did it in his own image. Everyone hustled, everyone strove and nearly everyone succeeded. Perhaps the greatest effort was put forth by Dave Parker, who silenced critics with his best season since his MVP days in Pittsburgh. Parker's 125 RBI nearly doubled that of the team's second-best run producer Nick Esasky, while Big Dave belted a career-high 34 homers and batted .312. Ron Oester also flourished, hitting .295, 34 points higher than his lifetime average.

But the strength of this Reds team lies in the bullpen, where John Franco and Ted Power emerged as the premier righty-lefty combination in baseball.

Dave Parker (facing page) raised the level of his play in 1985. Mario Soto (left) suffered through a sub-par season, while Pete Rose (above) looks at a second place finish.

They combined for 20 wins, 39 saves, posting an earned run average of well under 3.00.

The starting rotation was full of surprises. The first surprise was the 1-2 duo of Mario Soto and Jay Tibbs (traded in the off-season) who tallied a mere 22 wins between them. The second surprise was lefthander Tom Browning, who became the first rookie pitcher in three decades to win 20 games (even Dwight Gooden didn't do it!).

Still, there's no denying. When the talk concerns the Cincinnati Reds, the talk is usually about Pete Rose.

STADIUM: Riverfront Stadium. The Reds' ballpark replaced the old Crosley Field with the inaugural game held on June 30, 1970.

DIMENSIONS: 330 feet down the lines, 404 feet to centerfield.

TURF: Artificial.

CAPACITY: 52,392.

Speedster Vince
Coleman (main picture)
stole only one base
against the Dodgers in
the NLCS. When Tommy
Lasorda (inset top right)
moved Pedro Guerrero
to leftfield, the Dodgers
took off. Mike Marshall
(inset top left) had his
best season, while
Fernando Valenzuela
(inset bottom right)
continued to shine for
L.A.

Los Angeles Dodgers

For the first two months of the '85 season, the Dodgers resembled the bumbling 1962 expansion Mets. Routine ground balls were booted, fly balls were dropped and cutoffs were missed. After 46 games Los Angeles fielders committed 62 errors and were the laugh of the league. Then came June. Manager Tom Lasorda moved Pedro Guerrero to the outfield, rookie Mariano Duncan to shortstop and the Dodgers to the pennant.

Steve Sax (above) prospered after moving to the eighth slot. Bob Welch (top far right) was outstanding following an early injury. Pedro Guerrero (top right) finished second in the N.L. in hitting.

Guerrero rewarded Lasorde by responding with his best offensive season of his career, batting .320 with 33 home runs. Mike Marshall followed Guerrero's lead by clouting 28 homers and driving in 95 runs; Mike Scioscia rang

up the best numbers for a Dodgers catcher since Roy Campanella; and Greg Brock finally realized the potential the Dodgers felt he possessed by hitting 21 round-trippers.

But the backbone of this Dodgers team, like its predecessors, proved to be pitching. Los Angeles was the only team in the majors to post an earned run average of under 3.00 while the team's four starters, Fernando Valenzuela, Orel Hershiser, Bob Welch and Jerry Reuss combined to win 64 games against only 27 losses. The bullpen was almost as good as Tom Niedenfuer returned from an arm injury to record 19 saves.

And by the end of the season, it became apparent that the Dodgers had transformed themselves from the inept '62 Mets to the '69 World Championship version.

STADIUM: Dodger Stadium. The Los Angeles Dodgers' home is one of the most picturesque in baseball, with a backdrop of the Chavez Ravine beyond the outfield fences.

DIMENSIONS: 330 feet down the lines, 395 to centerfield.

TURF: Natural grass.

CAPACITY: 56,000.

Houston Astros

If nothing else, the Houston Astros are the most consistent team in baseball. They always get off to a horrible start, they always finish with a flourish and they always seem to finish around early, caught fire late and won 83 games to place third in the West.

On a team as consistent as the Astros, no player is more consistent than Jose Cruz. Cruz, a lifetime .300 hitter, batted – that's right – .300 and knocked in 79 runs with nine homers. He encountered plenty of company on the basepaths as the Astros finished second in the league in hitting and runs scored and first in base hits.

The young players Houston counted on blossomed nicely to give the Astros a solid core for the future. Bill Doran displayed his all-around ability by hitting .287 with 14 home runs and 59 RBI. Glenn Davis, brought up from the minors in mid-season, clouted 20 homers and drove in 64 in only 350 at-bats.

Where the Astros failed was on the mound. Despite an outstanding season from Mike Scott (18-8, 3.29 earned run average), the starters were unsteady. Nolan Ryan notched career strikeout number 4,000, but other than that

Pedro Guerrero's (facing page) move from third base to the outfield increased production from his bat. Jose Cruz (above) keeps his bat and average high as he leads the Astros.

milestone, his season was forgettable. Bob Knepper endured difficulties despite winning 15 games and Joe Niekro was ineffective most of the season and found himself with his brother Phil in a Yankees uniform by season's end.

One of the positive notes on the staff was the performance of the short relief man Dave Smith. The stocky righthander rebounded from arm and back woes to record 27 saves, a career best. Besides Smith, the rest of the bullpen was consistently inconsistent.

But then, what else would you expect from the Astros?

STADIUM: Astrodome. The Houston Astrodome was the world's first indoor, air-conditioned domed stadium, called the "Eighth Wonder of the World." The most difficult ballpark in the major leagues to hit home runs.

DIMENSIONS: 330 down the lines, 400 to centerfield.

TURF: Artificial.

CAPACITY: 45,000.

Atlanta Braves

Ever since Atlanta Braves games have been broadcast over owner Ted Turner's Superstation TBS, the Braves have adopted the nickname America's Team. With millions of viewers privy to Braves telecasts, the team has become the Dallas Cowboys of baseball. But if their recent woes on the field continue, Atlanta may be known as South America's team, because south is where they are headed in the standings.

Despite early-season optimism, the Braves tumbled long and hard in 1985, finishing fifth, just above the lowly Giants. And the reasons for the fall are clear; hitting, pitching and managing.

First the managing. After serving in the Atlanta organization since 1958, Eddie Haas took over the big club and only lasted half a season. To put it mildly, the team failed to respond to him and Turner responded by firing Haas in mid-season.

Second, the pitching. The Braves' staff compiled a plethora of negative statistics. Worst earned run average, fewest complete games, most hits, walks and home runs allowed. The only consistent starter was Rick Mahler, who also happened to be the only starter to win more than 10 games. Bruce Sutter signed a megabucks contract to provide relief, but he compiled the worst season of his career while suffering a shoulder injury late in the year.

Third, the hitting. Yes, Dale Murphy led the National League in homers (37) and knocked in 117 runs with a .300 average. Yes, Bob Horner produced healthy Bob Horner numbers with 27 home runs and 89 RBI. After those two, however, it's all downhill. The braves finished with the third lowest team batting average and found scoring runs a hardship.

STADIUM: Atlanta Fulton-County Stadium – Atlanta's stadium is known as one of the better hitter's parks in baseball.

TURF: Natural grass.

CAPACITY: 53,046

San Diego Padres

The San Diego Padres felt 1985 was the year to make a stand and it cost them where it hurt most – in the standings. Early in the season club president Ballard Smith refused to allow Alan Wiggins back after the speedy second baseman bolted following a drug relapse. After weeks of

negotiations, Smith finally dealt Wiggins to Baltimore. What Smith failed to realize was the importance of Wiggins to the Padres' offense.

With Wiggins in the lineup, San Diego steamrollered to the 1984 World Series. Without him, the Padres not only possessed the slowest team in baseball, but barely played .500 ball and crawled home a lowly fourth in the West.

The loss of Wiggins affected everyone in the lineup, but none more than Tony Gwynn. Gwynn, the major-league batting leader in '84, saw fewer fastballs without Wiggins on base in front of him and ultimately saw his production fall considerably. And without the tablesetters creating havoc, the tableclearers, Steve Garvey, Terry Kennedy, Kevin McReynolds and Carmelo Martinez, also suffered.

Andy Hawkins (right), Bob Horner (below) and Steve Garvey (bottom right) enjoyed fine seasons. Nolan Ryan (facing page) reached 4,000 strikeouts in '85.

The lack of run production hurt the pitching staff and forced them to carry much of the burden. LaMarr Hoyt, brought to the Padres in a trade, started slowly, came on strong and then succumbed to arm problems late in the season. Goose Gossage proved he wasn't over the hill by registering 26 saves and a tiny 1.82 earned run average. The most talked-about member of the staff in 1985 was unquestionably Eric Show, who hurled the famous pitch Pete Rose hit for the tie-breaking single and then pouted about it.

All in all, it was a season the Padres would like to forget – on and off the field.

STADIUM: Jack Murphy Stadium. The Padres' home opened on April 5, 1968 and now is considered one of the most pleasant parks in baseball to view a game.

DIMENSIONS: 330 feet down the lines, 405 feet to centerfield.

TURF: Natural grass.

CAPACITY: 58,671

S F Giants

Terry Kennedy (left) of the San Diego Padres hit 10 home runs and drove in 74 runs. Dave Dravecky (above) proved to be one of the steadiest starters for the Padres.

Throughout the Giants' history, they have been known to develop young, fleet, power-hitting outfielders. Through their system have passed such luminaries as Willie Mays, Bobby Bonds and George Foster. Beginning the 1985 season, Giants management felt it had another array of outfield stars in Chili Davis, Jeff Leonard and Dan Gladden on which to build a contender. Fast and powerful, the trio would lead San Francisco back to the top in the West.

Graig Nettles (left) turned in another solid year for the Padres at age 41. Jack Clark's (below) sweet swing was missed by the Giants.

But things didn't quite develop as expected. Gladden, a super rookie in 1984, turned into a sour sophomore. Leonard reversed field with his worst season as a Giant and Davis simply got caught in the mediocrity. It all added up to the worst season the Giants have recorded since moving to San Francisco and the first 100-loss campaign in the Bay area.

It gets worse. Fan attendance dropped better than 20 percent and the Giants drew only slightly more than 800,000 fans, the largest drop-off in the league.

Hitting proved the main problem in reaching all the aforementioned negatives. Besides the outfielders, others

registered disappointing seasons. David Green, brought to San Francisco in the Jack Clark trade, finished with less runs batted in than Clark did homers (22-20). In fact, no starter hit over in the major leagues.

The pitching furnished the only positive sign for the future. The bullpen duo of Scott Garrelts (9-6, 13 saves and a 2.30 earned run average) and Mark Davis (more strikeouts than any reliever in baseball) turned into an effective unit, while none of the starting pitchers could register a winning record.

What the Giants could use is a Willie Mays or a Bobby Bonds. With that team, though, they probably would need both.

STADIUM: Candlestick Park. The Giants' home is considered to be the worst ballpark in the major leagues to both play and view a game in. The chilling, gusting

winds coming off the Bay provide a wintry atmosphere even in July.

DIMENSIONS: 335 feet to leftfield, 400 feet to center, 330 feet to rightfield.

TURF: Natural grass.

CAPACITY: 58,000

Toronto Blue Jays

When Toronto general manager Pat Gillick evaluated his team's roster prior to last season, the obvious need for the Blue Jays was to shore up their impotent bullpen. So Gillick went out and acquired relievers Bill Caudill and Gary Lavelle and suddenly the experts predicted a first-place finish in the tough American League East. While the Fourth Estate was

George Bell (above and above left) came through with big numbers for the Jays, hitting 28 HRs with 95 RBI. Damasco Garcia (facing page) was no slouch either, batting .282 with 65 RBI.

right about the effect (the Jays won 99 games en route to the division title), they were wrong about the cause.

Caudill, who saved 89 games in the '80s, suffered through a lackluster season and registered just 14 saves, while Lavelle also proved ineffective (0 saves). But along on a white horse like the Canadian Mounted Police came Tom Henke a.k.a. The Terminator. All Henke did after arriving in mid-season was save 13 games, win four, post a 2.38 earned run average and use his 95 mile per hour fastball to become the bullpen stopper. Another major contributor to the pen was Dennis Lamp. A disappointment in

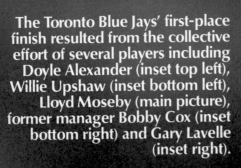

The Toronto Blue Jays' first-place finish resulted from the collective effort of several players including Doyle Alexander (inset top left), Willie Upshaw (inset bottom left), Lloyd Moseby (main picture), former manager Bobby Cox (inset bottom right) and Gary Lavelle (inset right).

1984, Lamp rebounded to record a perfect 11-0 slate in long relief.

Henke was not the only reason Toronto became the first non-American city ever to win a division title. Dave Stieb compiled a typical Stieb campaign, leading the league in earned run average (2.48) and starting in the All-Star game. Jimmy Key developed into an outstanding left-hander (14-6, 3.00 e.r.a. and a berth on the All-Star team) and Doyle Alexander turned in another fine season by registering a 17-10 slate.

Dave Stieb (above) won only 14 games for the Jays, but once again started the All-Star game and captured the E.R.A. title for the first time. Lloyd Moseby (left) turned in an outstanding season, while Damasco Garcia (facing page) also distinguished himself.

The hitting proved another story. Many of the Blue Jay regulars experienced sub-par seasons, yet the Jays still won their division. Lloyd Moseby and Willie Upshaw led the way with a dip in average and power numbers. Only two players, George Bell (an American League MVP candidate until a poor September spoiled his chances) and Jesse Barfield, produced truly outstanding offensive numbers while Tony Fernandez turned into one of the finest shortstops in the majors.

Still, if it wasn't for the improved bullpen, the Jays may have taken home the second prize in the East again.

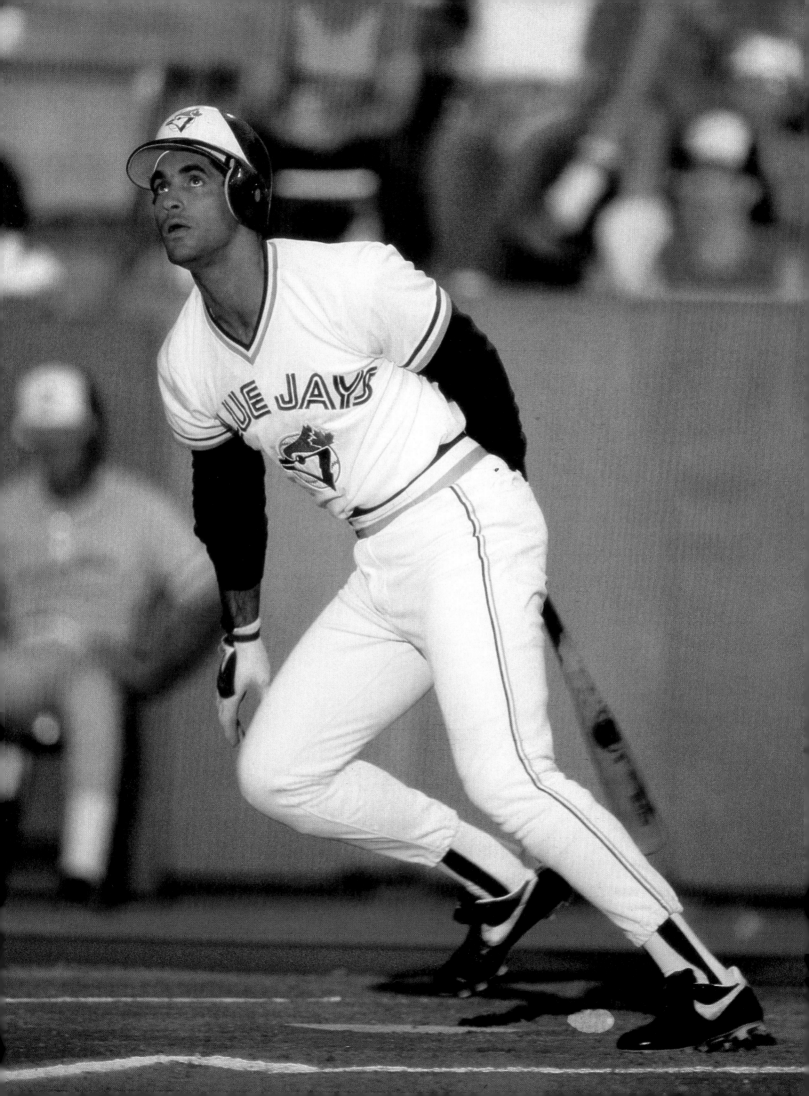

STADIUM: Exhibition Stadium. The nine-year-old Toronto stadium is located on the grounds of Exhibition Place, a 350-acre complex visited by millions each year.

DIMENSIONS: 330 feet down the lines, 400 feet to centerfield.

TURF: Artificial.

CAPACITY: 43,737.

New York Yankees

The Bronx Bombers returned to Yankee Stadium in 1985. While they may not be mistaken for the Murderers' Row of Gehrig, Ruth, Lazzari and Meusel, the 1985 version did pack the punch that had become the Yankee tradition. Led by American League Most Valuable Player Don Mattingly, the Yankees pushed

Dave Righetti (above) led a solid bullpen for the Yanks. Dave Winfield (facing page) contributed his ususal hustle.

across more runs than any team in baseball.

When discussing the hitting exploits of the Yanks, the conversation always begins with Mattingly. The 25-year-old first baseman, who won the batting title in his second season, responded with an even more productive third campaign. He became the first Yankee since Joe DiMaggio to collect a pair of 200 hit seasons in a row. Besides hitting .324 Mattingly clouted 35 homers and knocked in 145 runs, the most by a major leaguer since Ted Williams.

Mattingly also had company at the plate. Dave Winfield compiled another outstanding season with 26 homers and 114 RBI to go along with another Gold Glove. Don Baylor disdained batting average for power (.231) and recorded 91 ribbies and 23 round-trippers. Even the leadoff hitter, Rickey Henderson, got in on the power act. Henderson socked 24 homers, drove in 72 runs and hit .314 to go with his usual stolen base crown (80) and havoc on the basepaths. Add those four to Mike Pagliarulo (19 HR, 62 RBI) and Ken Griffey (.274, 10 HR, 69 RBI) and you have one potent attack.

The pitching staff proved a surprise by attaining the third-best earned run

average among A.L. teams. Ron Guidry returned to his Cy Young form (he placed second in the voting), winning 22 games while Phil Niekro, at age 46, chipped in 16 wins, his last being career victory number 300.

The bullpen also pulled its weight. Dave Righetti wavered at times, but still managed 29 saves, 12 wins and a 2.78 e.r.a. The biggest surprise was the emergence of rookie Brian Fisher. Fisher, 22, came to the Yankees in the Rick Cerone deal and immediately paid dividends. He settled into the role of right-handed stopper, winning four, saving 14 with a sparkling 2.38 e.r.a.

Still, the calling card of the Yankees was hitting. Just like it used to be.

A number of Yankees spent much time on the basepaths, including Rickey Henderson (left), A.L. M.V.P. Don Mattingly (bottom left) and Dave Winfield (bottom right). Ron Guidry (facing page) won 20 games for the third time.

STADIUM: Yankee Stadium. The House that Ruth Built is best known for its short porch in rightfield, a paradise for left-handed sluggers, and purgatory for right-handed pitchers.

DIMENSIONS: 312 to leftfield, 417 to centerfield, 310 feet to rightfield.

TURF: Natural grass.

CAPACITY: 57,545.

Detroit Tigers

When the Detroit Tigers jumped out of the gate with a 35-5 record in 1984 and went on to win the World Championship, manager Sparky Anderson quickly proclaimed the Tigers a dynasty-to-be. Anderson further opined that the Tigers, man-for-man, were better than Sparky's last championship squad, the "Big Red Machine" of the mid-'70s.

Maybe the Tigers read those quotes and decided they didn't have to play as hard. Or maybe Anderson misjudged the talent, because the Tigers slipped badly in 1985, placing third in the A.L. East, 15 games behind the division winning Blue Jays.

Whatever the reason, hitting was not a problem for Detroit. Kirk Gibson finished his best season, leading the Tigers in batting average (.287) while smashing 29 home runs and knocking in 97 runs. Lou Whitaker further enhanced his reputation as the major league's best second baseman, hitting .273 with 21 homers, 73 RBI and snaring another Gold Glove. The offense also possessed Darrell Evans, the major league home run champ who clouted 40 round-trippers and Lance Parrish who added 28 homers and 98 RBI.

The pitching was another story. The Tigers staff topped the A.L. in its championship season, but staggered badly last year. Perhaps the number one culprit was Milt Wilcox. The veteran right-hander and third starter pitched only eight games due to injury, winning one of four decisions. Willie Hernandez, the A.L. M.V.P. and Cy Young hurler in 1984, proved hittable, although his stats were impressive (.31 saves, 2.70 earned run average).

Still, the Tigers proved they aren't as good as the "Big Red Machine." Even Sparky Anderson will have to admit that.

The Tigers all-star catcher Lance Parrish (facing page) and slugging rightfielder Kirk Gibson (left) provided the Detroit offense with punch.

STADIUM: Tiger Stadium. Another of the old, cozy American League parks, Tiger Stadium is a hitter's paradise, especially with the overhang in rightfield.

DIMENSIONS: 340 feet to leftfield, 440 feet to centerfield, 325 feet to rightfield.

TURF: Natural grass.

CAPACITY: 52,806.

Baltimore Orioles

The Baltimore Orioles may have the finest pitching tradition of any team in the major leagues. Luminaries such as Jim Palmer, Mike Cuellar and Dave McNally have donned the Birds' uniform and, along with Pat Dobson, were the last staff

Dan Petry (left) and Kirk Gibson of Detroit (above) and Eddie Murray of Baltimore (facing page) starred in 1985.

to have four 20-game winners. Recently, the Orioles successfully passed on the torch of pitching excellence to the likes of Mike Boddicker, Scott McGregor and Mike Flanagan, to name a few. But in 1985, the torch flickered and finally blew out. It meant a porous fourth place finish for the Birds, their fewest number of victories since 1972, and the return of Earl Weaver for the ousted Joe Altobelli.

The Orioles' pitching staff posted a collective 4.38 earned run average, the seventh worst in the league. Of their top four starters, none managed an e.r.a. of under 4.00. Boddicker, a 20-game winner the previous season, won only 12, lost 17 and allowed 227 hits in 203.1 innings. McGregor compiled a 14-14 mark but he, too, yielded an unusually high number of hits-to-innings-pitched ratio. Flanagan, injured most of the season, returned to the tune of 4-5 with a 5.13 e.r.a.

It's a shame the O's encountered such difficulty pitching because their hitting produced a major league leading 212 home runs.

Eddie Murray, of course, led the way, smacking 31 home runs, knocking in 124 runs and batting .297. Cal Ripken, who continued his amazing streak of 5,545 consecutive innings played, contributed 26 dingers and 110 RBI. Free-agent pick-up Fred Lynn kicked in 23 homers and 68 RBI, while Michael Young assumed the designated hitter slot and belted 28 round-trippers and 81 ribbies

Unfortunately for the Orioles, poor pitching doomed their chances. And they hope it doesn't become a tradition.

STADIUM: Memorial Stadium.

TURF: Natural grass.

CAPACITY: 53,198.

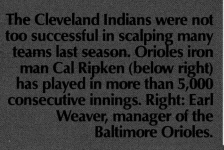

The Cleveland Indians were not too successful in scalping many teams last season. Orioles iron man Cal Ripken (below right) has played in more than 5,000 consecutive innings. Right: Earl Weaver, manager of the Baltimore Orioles.

Cleveland Indians

Being a Cleveland Indians fan is not easy. After all, the Indians do not exactly have the most glamorous history. Consider the Indians' last pennant winner was in 1954. They've finished no higher than third place five times since. And their 60-102 record of futility in 1985 tied the second lowest winning percentage in Cleveland history. Need any more proof?

One glance at the Indians' pitching staff will show why Cleveland finished 39½ lengths behind Toronto. The Indians' staff dropped to the bottom in earned run average (4.91) and saves. They owned the dubious honor of being first in the American League in hits allowed, runs yielded and hit batsmen. Any way you look at it, the Indians were a disgrace.

The Cleveland hitting, however, proved the antithesis of its pitching peers. Leadoff hitter Brett Butler placed fifth in the A.L. batting race, averaging .311 with five homers, 50 RBI and 47 stolen bases. Julio Franco once again helped set the standard for hitting shortstops (with Cal Ripken) by knocking in 90 runs and batting .288. Brook Jacoby settled in nicely to the third base position, hitting .274 with 20 homers and 87 ribbies. Andre Thornton suffered through an off-season despite clouting 22 homers and driving in a team-high 88 runs.

But any way you look at the Indians they're still a last-place team. Just ask any of their fans.

STADIUM: Cleveland Stadium.

DIMENSIONS: 320 feet down the lines, 400 feet to centerfield.

TURF: Natural grass.

CAPACITY: 74,208.

Boston Red Sox

A look at the Boston Red Sox statistics confirms how important pitching is in baseball. The Sox led the major leagues in batting with a .282 team average and scored nearly five runs per game. Still, the Sox finished fifth, 18½ games behind the Jays with an 81-81 slate.

Much of Boston's problems had to do with its pitching staff. The cumulative earned run average was 4.06 and the Red Sox had only two pitchers, Dennis "Oil Can" Boyd and Bruce Hurst, who finished

Cleveland Indians fans (facing page) didn't have much to cheer about. Tony Armas' (above) production fell and Dennis "Oil Can" Boyd (right) came to the fore.

in double figures in victories. Roger Clemens, thought of as the Boston stopper, made only 15 starts due to an ailing shoulder. The bullpen lacked a real closer as Steve Crawford led the pen with only 12 saves. The Red Sox realized their deficiency in relief by acquiring Wes Gardner from the Mets, a successful "closer" in the minor leagues and Sammy Stewart from the Orioles in the off-season.

As sour as the pitching, that's how sweet the Red Sox batters were in 1985. Wade Boggs finished a magical season with 240 hits and a .368 average to win the batting title. Bill Buckner continues to

Manager John McNamara (inset top left) shows the strain of a fifth-place finish. Jackie Gutierrez (inset bottom left) was traded after hitting only .218. Jim Rice (main picture) continued his assault on A.L. pitchers with 27 homers. Wade Boggs (inset right) won his second batting title.

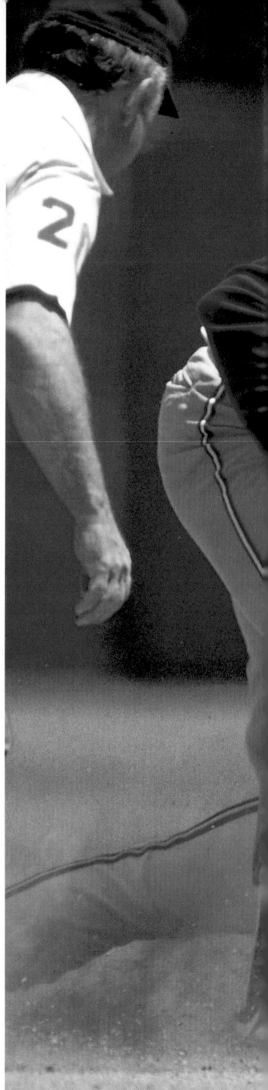

get better with age, posting a .299 average with 16 homers and 110 RBI. Jim Rice grounded into a record number of double plays, yet hit 27 homers and knocked in 103 runs. And Tony Armas, the 1984 home run king, clouted only 23 round-trippers and 64 RBI due to injuries.

Despite the outstanding offensive production by the Sox, it's clear pitching wins pennants. Just ask the Toronto Blue Jays.

STADIUM: Fenway Park. The Red Sox home is perhaps the most distinctive in the major leagues, with the famed "Green Monster", a 37-foot wall in leftfield, the feature. Constructed in 1912, the park is a fan's delight, as the players seem a heart-beat away in almost every seat.

DIMENSIONS: 315 feet to leftfield, 420 feet to centerfield, 302 feet to rightfield.

TURF: Natural grass.

CAPACITY: 33,583.

George Brett (above), the Royals' "Mr. Everything", readies himself at third base. Cleveland's Pat Tabler (right) slides hard into second base.

Kansas City Royals

When the Kansas City Royals began the 1985 season, manager Dick Howser had no delusions of grandeur. He knew the Royals were a team with many holes, especially on offense. There was no pure clean-up hitter, the shortstop situation was unstable at best and George Brett was coming off his least productive major league campaign. But Howser relied on a young, talented pitching staff, a solid defense and a rejuvenated Brett to capture, in dramatic fashion, the division title, the league championship and ultimately the World Championship.

And no player had more to do with it than Brett. After another injury-plagued season in 1984, Brett went on a rigorous

Charlie Leibrandt (inset left) surprised many by winning 17 games for K.C. Willie Wilson (inset bottom left) made a successful comeback while Hal McRae (main picture) successfully hung on.

off-season training program that helped him to play in 155 games and to perhaps his finest season.

The perennial all-star placed second in the batting race with a .335 average, belted a career-high 30 home runs and drove in 112 runs. He also walked 31 times intentionally, a tribute to his hitting skills.

Brett did have some company at the plate. Steve Balboni batted only .243, but supplied the power with 36 homers and 88 runs batted in. Frank White, known earlier in his career for his fielding exploits, became a clean-up hitter out of necessity and responded with 22 round-trippers.

But the most important part of the team was the pitching staff. Bret Saberhagen emerged as the American League's premier pitcher, compiling a 20-6 record with a 2.87 earned run average. Charlie Leibrandt kicked in with his finest season, winning 17 with an e.r.a. of 2.69. And Danny Jackson, Mark Gubicza and Bud Black provided excellent depth in the rotation as the trio registered 38 wins among them. As usual, Dan Quisenberry led the bullpen with 37 saves and a 2.37 e.r.a.

Yet despite all the Royals' shortcomings, Howser was able to piece together a fine squad. Make that a championship squad.

STADIUM: Royals Stadium. The World Champions' ballpark is more typical of a National League stadium with its artificial turf, huge gaps and symmetrical dimensions. The water spectacular, running from centerfield to the rightfield corner, is renowned for its beauty.

DIMENSIONS: 330 feet down the lines, 410 feet to centerfield.

TURF: Artificial.

CAPACITY: 40,625.

Milwaukee Brewers

When George Bamberger agreed to unretire and take the reins of the Milwaukee Brewers, he knew his biggest problem would be reconstructing the beleaguered pitching staff. And after one season, Bamberger knows it's not going to be a simple task.

The Brewers once again landed in the bottom half of the pitching charts with only one hurler, Ted Higuera, posting more that 10 wins. None of the other

Mark Gubicza (facing page) pitched in to help the Royals to the championship as manager Dick Howser (right) guided them.

starters even compiled a winning record as the Brewers were victors only 71 times in 1985.

Bamberger realized the need to start over and in the off-season the Brewers dropped two pitchers who figured prominently in their 1982 World Series appearance. Exit Pete Vuckovich, a Cy Young winner in 1982, and former ace reliever Rollie Fingers. Both were cut from the roster after experiencing horrid seasons. Enter the young arms, Tim Leary and Jamie Coconower, unproven, yet bursting with talent.

Two former stars, Robin Yount and Paul Molitor, returned from injuries to compile reasonably good statistics. Yount, recovering from shoulder miseries, moved to left-field from shortstop and hit

.277 with 15 home runs and 68 runs batted in. Molitor, meanwhile, led the team in batting (.297) and stolen bases (21). Cecil Cooper proved skeptics who felt his career was over wrong by hitting .292 with 16 homers and 99 RBI, and Earnest Riles leapfrogged to the head of the rookie class by hitting .286 with 5 homers and 45 ribbies.

But Bamberger knows winners start with a strong pitching staff. And the Brewers aren't winners...yet.

STADIUM: Milwaukee County Stadium.

DIMENSIONS: 315 feet down the lines, 402 feet to centerfield.

TURF: Natural grass.

CAPACITY: 53,192

California Angels

Gene Mauch has been a manager in the major leagues 24 years and still hasn't won a pennant. Maybe that's why the California Angels' second-place finish in the West didn't surprise anyone – even though they led most of the season and held first place until the final week of the season. Still, the Angels won 91 games and finished only one game behind the eventual World Champion Royals.

Perhaps the most pleasant aspect of the Angels' win total is that it may be just

The Royals slid by the Blue Jays (previous page main picture) all season. Mark Gubicza's (previous pages inset top left) explosive fastball made Willie Wilson (previous pages inset top right) smile all season. Bret Saberhagen (previous pages inset bottom) emerged as the staff stopper. The Brewers argued (top) more than they won. George Brett (left) remained the heart and soul of the Royals. Brian Downing (facing page) paced the Angels attack with 85 RBI.

the start of many winning seasons to come. The pitching staff, which carried the club, is young and improving. Mike Witt, who hurled a perfect game the last day of the 1984 regular season, continued his progress by winning 15 of 24 decisions with a 3.56 earned run average. Youngsters Rom Romanick (25) and Kirk McCaskill (25) won 14 and 12 games respectively, while "senior citizen" Don Sutton, 40, recorded a 15-10 slate. Add those four to John Candelaria (a late-season acquisition) and you have a fine rotation. The bullpen wasn't too shabby either as Donnie Moore surprisingly saved 31 games, won eight and registered a sparkling 1.92 e.r.a.

It's not too hard to figure out why the Angels didn't win their division when you look at their attack.

California finished dead-last in team batting (.252) and only one regular

topped the .300 mark. Reggie Jackson proved critics wrong again by clouting 27 home runs and driving in 85 runs to lead the Angels in those categories. Rod Carew did manage to get his 3,000th hit, yet his .280 average was his worst in the major leagues since his sophomore campaign.

Maybe in Gene Mauch's silver anniversary as a skipper he'll be able to bring home some silverware.

STADIUM: Anaheim Stadium.

DIMENSIONS: 333 feet down the lines, 404 feet to centerfield.

TURF: Natural grass.

CAPACITY: 65,158.

Chicago White Sox

When the Chicago White Sox traded former Cy Young award winner LaMarr Hoyt to San Diego in exchange for minor-league shortstop Ozzie Guillen (they were the principals), the Sox braintrust was heavily inundated with second-guessers. But after just one season, the skeptics have been quelled by a little Venezuelan shortstop with the first name synonymous with fielding excellence.

Ozzie Guillen not only won the American League Rookie-of-the-Year, but also helped the Sox attain the distinction of committing the smallest number of errors in the A.L. And while fielding has always been Guillen's forte, he responded at the bat, surprising many by hitting .273. Carlton Fisk, the Sox backstop, also surprised many by

cracking a career high 37 homers and 107 runs batted in. One hitter who wasn't surprising was Harold Baines. The 27-year-old Baines put it all together in 1985, slamming 22 homers, knocking in 113 runs and batting .309, sixth best in the league.

On the pitching side, Tom Seaver won his 300th in an emotional return to New York and proved to be the stopper on the staff, compiling a 16-11 record with a 3.77 earned run average. Britt Burns, traded to the Yankees over the winter, overcame his usual physical problems to go 18-11. The big negative in the rotation, though, was losing Rich Dotson (3-4, 4.47 e.r.a.) to an injury early in the season.

Reggie Jackson (below) and Doug DeCinces (facing page) led the Angels' attack. Tom Seaver (below left) won number 300.

seemingly blew just as many opportunities and finished the season with a bloated 3.48 earned run average.

Thankfully, the starters were a little more reliable than the bullpen. Bert Blyleven, obtained for the stretch drive, compiled an overall record of 17-16 with a 3.16 e.r.a. and as usual was consistently good. Frank Viola, who yielded Rod Carew's 3,000th hit, finished the season with a respectable 18-14 record, while Mike Smithson and John Butcher combined for 26 victories.

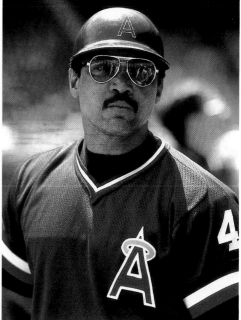

Manager Gene Mauch (left) failed to bring home a winner again. Reggie Jackson (above) proved he's not finished by clouting a team-high 27 HRs. Carlton Fisk (facing page) tags out Tony Fernandez. Greg Walker (overleaf inset left) had his best season in the majors as did teammate Harold Baines (overleaf inset right). Carlton Fisk (overleaf main picture) was in his share of home plate collisions.

Bob James, acquired for second baseman Vance Law in 1984, provided relief out of the bullpen, winning eight games, saving a career-high 32 and posting a 2.13 e.r.a.

If nothing else, 1985 was a good trading season for the White Sox. Good enough for third place, at least.

STADIUM: Comiskey Park. The White Sox' stadium holds the distinction of being the nation's oldest active ballpark, opened July 1, 1910.

DIMENSIONS: 341 feet down the lines, 401 feet to centerfield.

TURF: Natural grass.

CAPACITY: 44,432.

Minnesota Twins

Playing in the American League's only indoor stadium with poor lighting and poor visibility, it's no wonder the Minnesota Twins often played like a Jekyll and Hyde team. Throughout the season, the Twins were consistent in their inconsistency, and they proved to be the "streakiest" squad in the league. Win eight, lose six, win four, lose eight. That's the way the 1985 season went for the Twins.

No part of the team was more inconsistent than the pitching staff and no pitcher on the staff was more inconsistent than bullpen ace Ron Davis. Davis led the team in saves with 25, yet

The Twins have always been identified as a hitting team and the 1985 version of the Twins helped keep that lore intact. Kent Hrbek struggled early with injuries, but a late surge moved his numbers to what they should be (.278, 21 homers, 93 RBI). Tom Brunansky clobbered 27 homers and knocked in 90 runs, while Gary Gaetti chipped in with 20 round-trippers. Kirby Puckett scored 80 runs from the leadoff slot, batted .288 and played a flawless centerfield. Perhaps the biggest surprise was Mark Salas, who did a fine job behind the plate and hit .300 to boot.

All in all, it was a Jekyll-Hyde season for the Twins. Maybe next season they'll find out which way to go.

STADIUM: Hubert H. Humphrey Metrodome. Opened in 1981, the Metrodome is one of two American League indoor parks. It is noted for its poor lighting, causing many a fielder to "lose" a fly ball, and its rock-hard surface, which has resulted in unnatural hops in the outfield.

DIMENSIONS: 343 feet to leftfield, 408 feet to centerfield, 327 feet to rightfield.

TURF: Artificial.

CAPACITY: 55,122.

Oakland Athletics

It's hard to believe that just five short years ago the Oakland A's were one of the better teams in baseball. Tony Armas, Rickey Henderson and Dwayne Murphy comprised the most exciting and arguably the best outfield in the major leagues, and the young pitching staff prospered under the guidance of Billy Martin.

But trades sent Armas and Henderson away and the rotation crumbled under the enormous workload. What's left is a middle-of-the-road team that finished tied for fourth place with Minnesota in the weak A.L. West Division.

The trade of Henderson, though, brought a wealth of young pitching prospects. Jay Howell stepped in and immediately became the bullpen ace, saving 29 games and being named as an All-Star. Jose Rijo, at the age of 20, won six games in limited service and tendered an earned run average of 3.53. Tim Birtsas, the third pitcher in the Henderson deal, posted a 10-6 record and the mark of a promising future. Chris Codiroli proved to be the staff's top winner with 14 victories despite a high e.r.a. of 4.46.

Kent Hrbek (facing page) started slowly but finished with a bang. Ron Davis (left) was very inconsistent as the relief ace. Frank Viola (below left) won 18 games for the Twins.

Dave Kingman (left) came through with his usual power display for the A's. Donnie Hill (main picture) jumps to avoid a collision at second base.

On the hitting front, Mike Davis paced the attack, batting .287 with 24 homers and 82 RBI. Dave Kingman contributed his usual 30 home runs and 91 RBI while Murphy, who won another Gold Glove, fell off offensively, hitting a team-low .233 with 20 round-trippers and only 59 ribbies. Alfredo Griffin batted .270, drove in 64 runs and collected a Gold Glove, and Carney Lansford suffered through an off-year, knocking in just 46 runs.

It's a shame the A's were just an average team because they could have been much better.

STADIUM: Oakland-Alameda County Coliseum. The A's home is considered a long-ball stadium, suited for power hitters.

DIMENSIONS: 330 feet down the lines, 397 feet to centerfield.

TURF: Natural grass.

CAPACITY: 50,255.

Oakland's Carney Lansford (above left) and Dwayne Murphy (facing page) suffered through poor offensive seasons, while Dave Henderson (above) and Alvin Davis (left) tried to put Seattle on the map.

Seattle Mariners

Mention the words Seattle Mariners to some baseball fans and you'll probably get a blank stare. That's how unknown the Mariners are and one of the team's biggest problems is its identity. Yet if you take a long look at the Mariners' roster, the future does not look so anonymous.

Although Seattle finished sixth in the West, the Mariners possessed a bunch of young players who seem destined for stardom. Phil Bradley, in only his second full season, nearly rewrote the Mariners' record book. The 27-year-old outfielder set club marks in hits (192), total bases (319) and extra base hits (67), while leading the regulars in batting (.300) and runs batted in (88). Alvin Davis, the American League Rookie-of-the-Year in 1984, rebounded from a difficult start to bat .287 with 18 homers and 78 RBI. Jim Presley, in his first full major league season, compiled the finest year ever by a Mariners third baseman, hitting .275 with 28 home runs and 84 RBI. And Gorman Thomas recovered from a rotator cuff injury to round out the offense with 32 round-trippers and 87 ribbies.

The pitching staff also possess a

Texas Rangers

The more things change, the more they stay the same. That cliche may be old, but it fits no team in the major leagues better than the Texas Rangers. For years, the Rangers have been the A.L. West doormat and in 1985, they enhanced their reputation by losing 99 games and finishing dead-last, 28½ lengths behind the Royals.

batted .287 with 15 homers and 70 RBI and Pete O'Brien compiled his best numbers by hitting .267 with 22 home runs and 92 ribbies. But the biggest surprise was rookie center-fielder Oddibe McDowell. The 23-year-old speedster was called to the big club in mid-season and, after a dreadful start, batted .239 with 18 home runs and 42 RBI. He also stole 25 bases and played a solid defensive game.

But any way you look at the Rangers

wealth of young talent. Mike Moore, 26, topped the staff by winning 17, losing 10 with a respectable 3.46 earned run average. Mark Langston, A.L. Rookie Pitcher of the Year and strikeout leader in '84, struggled through an injury-riddled sophomore campaign that saw him fall to 7-14. Matt Young also encountered difficulties in his third Mariners' season, yet managed to win 12 games. The bullpen, headed by Edwin Nunez and Karl Best, showed much potential.

If all of those young players develop as they should, maybe the mention of the name Mariners some day will mean something.

STADIUM: Kingdome. The Mariners' indoor facility was opened April 9, 1976. Its 23-foot right-field wall is the majors' second-highest outfield fence behind the "Green Monster" at Fenway Park.

DIMENSIONS: 316 feet down the lines, 410 feet to centerfield.

TURF: Artificial.

CAPACITY: 59,438.

It didn't take long for the Rangers' season to turn upside-down. Doug Rader, given an extension prior to the season, lasted only a couple of months as Bobby Valentine was imported from the Mets' third base coaching box to take over. But even Valentine's enthusiastic approach couldn't help the Rangers salvage the campaign.

The main problem area of Texas was the pitching staff. The Rangers held the dubious distinction of yielding the most home runs in the A.L., compiling the fewest shutouts and registering the third highest earned run average. Only Charlie Hough could muster more than 10 victories and Hough, the ancient knuckleballer, won 14 while allowing 3.31 runs per nine innings. Greg Harris also stepped to the fore in the bullpen, going 5-4 with 11 saves and a 2.47 earned run average.

The Rangers offense proved a perfect match for the porous pitching staff as Texas finished last in runs scored, hits, doubles and RBI.

Only a handful of players were able to put any spark into the club. Gary Ward

Lee Lacy (top) slides in just ahead of the tag. Larry Parrish (facing page), who was injured much of the season, strides into one of his 17 home runs.

it's the same old thing. The more they change, the more they stay the same.

STADIUM: Arlington Stadium. The home of the Texas Rangers could be second to the Giants' Candlestick Park in terms of comfort as the sweltering summer heat bakes the players and the fans. It is also noted as one of baseball's best parks for home runs.

DIMENSIONS: 330 feet down the lines, 400 feet to centerfield.

TURF: Natural grass.

CAPACITY: 43,508.